First World War
and Army of Occupation
War Diary
France, Belgium and Germany

60 DIVISION
Divisional Troops
Loyal North Lancashire Regiment
12th Battalion Pioneers
21 June 1916 - 31 December 1916

WO95/3028/6

The Naval & Military Press Ltd
www.nmarchive.com
Published in association with The National Archives

Published by

The Naval & Military Press Ltd

Unit 10 Ridgewood Industrial Park,

Uckfield, East Sussex,

TN22 5QE England

Tel: +44 (0) 1825 749494

www.naval-military-press.com

www.nmarchive.com

This diary has been reprinted in facsimile from the original. Any imperfections are inevitably reproduced and the quality may fall short of modern type and cartographic standards.

© Crown Copyright
Images reproduced by permission of The National Archives, London, England, 2015.

Contents

Document type	Place/Title	Date From	Date To
Heading	WO95/3028/6		
Heading	1-12th Bn Loy. Nth Lancs (Pioneers) 1916 Jun-1916 Dec		
Heading	60 Division Divl Troops 1-12th Bn Loyal Nth Lancs Regt (Pioneers) 1916 June-Dec 1916		
Heading	War Diary Of 1/12th Bn Loyal North Lancs Regt (Pioneers) From 21st June 1916 To 30th June 1916 (Volume I)		
War Diary		21/06/1916	30/06/1916
Heading	War Diary Of 1/12th Bn, Loyal North Lancs Regt. (Pioneers) From 1st July 1916 To 31st July 1916		
War Diary		21/06/1916	30/06/1916
Heading	War Diary Of 1/12th Bn Loyal North Lancs Regt (Pioneers) From 1st July 1916 To 31st July 1916 (Volume 2)		
War Diary		01/07/1916	30/07/1916
Heading	War Diary Of 1/12th Bn Loyal North Lancs Regt (Pioneers) August 1st 1916 To August 31st 1916 (Volume 3)		
War Diary		01/08/1916	31/08/1916
Heading	War Diary Of 1/12th Bn Loyal North Lancs Regt. (Pioneers) August 1st 1916 To August 31st 1916 (Volume 3)		
War Diary		01/08/1916	31/08/1916
Heading	War Diary Of 1/12th Bn Loyal North Lancs Regt. (Pioneers) From 1st September 1916 To 30th September 1916 (Volume 4)		
War Diary		01/09/1916	27/09/1916
Heading	War Diary Of 1/12th Bn Loyal North Lancs Regt (Pioneers) From 1st September To 30th September 1916 (Volume 4)		
War Diary		01/09/1916	27/09/1916
Heading	War Diary Of 1/12th Bn Loyal North Lancs Regt (Pioneers) From 1st October To 31st October 1916 (Volume 5)		
War Diary		01/10/1916	31/10/1916
Heading	War Diary Of 1/12th Bn Loyal North Lancs Regt (Pioneers) From 1st October To 31st October 1916 (Volume 5)		
War Diary		01/10/1916	31/10/1916
Miscellaneous	32nd Divisional Pioneers Joined From 60th Division 16.11.16.	16/11/1916	16/11/1916
War Diary		01/11/1916	30/11/1916
Miscellaneous	32nd Divisional Pioneers		
Miscellaneous	To Headquarters 32 Division	01/01/1917	01/01/1917
Heading	War Diary of 1/12 Bn. Loyal North. Lancs Regt. (Pioneers) From 1st December To 31st December 1916 (Volume 7)		
War Diary		01/12/1916	31/12/1916

Heading	War Diary Of 1/12th Bn Loyal North Lancs Regt (Pioneers) From 1st November To 30th November 1916 (Volume 6)		
War Diary		01/11/1916	30/11/1916
Miscellaneous	To Colonel C/c T.F Record Preston	01/01/1917	01/01/1917
Heading	War Diary Of 1/12th Bn Loyal North Lancs Regt (Pioneers) From 1st December To 31st December 1916 (Volume 7)		
War Diary		01/12/1916	31/12/1916

WO 95/3028/6

60TH DIVISION

From UK

1-12TH BN LOY. NTH LANCS

(PIONEERS)

~~JUN OCT 1916~~

1916 JUN — 1916 DEC

To SALONIKA

60 DIV. TROOPS

60 DIVISION
DIVL TROOPS

1-12TH BN LOYAL NTH LANCS REGT
(PIONEERS)
1916 JUNE - DEC 1916

TO SALONIKA

Army Form C. 2118.

"P/30"

WAR DIARY
or
INTELLIGENCE SUMMARY

(Erase heading not required.)

Confidential.

War Diary
of
1/12th Bn. Loyal North Lancs Regt. (Pioneers)

from 21st June 1916 to 30th June 1916

(Volume I)

Army Form C. 2118.

WAR DIARY
or
INTELLIGENCE SUMMARY
(Erase heading not required.)

Instructions regarding War Diaries and Intelligence Summaries are contained in F. S. Regs., Part II. and the Staff Manual respectively. Title Pages will be prepared in manuscript.

Place	Date	Hour	Summary of Events and Information	Remarks and references to Appendices
	June 21		The battalion left SUTTON VENY CAMP, WARMINSTER, WILTSHIRE, in the early morning and embarked, less Transport, at SOUTHAMPTON, on the S.S. CESAREA, the Transport proceeding on the S.S. CITY of DUNKIRK.	
	June 22		Landed at HAVRE 7 am and proceeded to No 1 Rest Camp, POINT ST ADDRESSE. Landing Strength :- 31 Officers 852 Other Ranks.	
	June 23		The battalion spent the day resting, with the exception of "C" Company who spent the afternoon from 4 to 7 pm keeping order in the V.D Camp and 50 men of "B" company who spend the night on guard at the V.D Camp. Left HAVRE 9 pm.	
	June 24		Arrived ST POL 3 pm. Detrained and marched to TERNAS where we were billeted for the night.	
	June 25		We rested at TERNAS all morning and left there at 3 pm and marched from there on the main ST POL - ARRAS Road as far as HAUTE - AVESNES. From there, C and D Companies under Captain G.W. Parkinson proceeded to ACQ, and Headquarters with A and B Companies went on to LOUEZ where we arrived at 12-30 am on the 26th, the Transport being left at DUISANS. Both the detachments at ACQ and LOUEZ were billeted.	
	June 26		The whole battalion remained all day at billets. We are attached to the 1/8th Bn. Royal Scots (Pioneers), 51st Highland Division, to take over their duties.	
	June 27		The battalion took up its working positions this evening. "A" Company under Captain J.P. Bayley went into Reserve Trenches at ARIANE to work on the defence of ENTONNOIR under	

2449 Wt. W14957/M90 750,000 1/16 J.B.C. & A. Forms/C.2118/12.

Army Form C. 2118.

WAR DIARY
or
INTELLIGENCE SUMMARY
(Erase heading not required.)

Instructions regarding War Diaries and Intelligence Summaries are contained in F. S. Regs., Part II. and the Staff Manual respectively. Title Pages will be prepared in manuscript.

Place	Date	Hour	Summary of Events and Information	Remarks and references to Appendices
			The C.E. 17th Corps. One platoon of "B" Company under 2nd Lieut. J.E.S. Bodger to ARIANE on "B" work under the C.R.E. 51st Division. One platoon of "B" Company under 2nd Lieut. R. Hodgkinson at LA MAISON BLANCHE for work on the FORK REDOUBT. The company and half mentioned are all on the ARRAS-BETHUNE ROAD between ECURIE and NEUVILLE ST VAASTE. Two platoons of "B" Company made up to 120 men out of "A" company and under the command of Lieut. T.C.L. Yarrow with Lieut. J. Barton-Smith and 2nd Lieuts. P.P. Butler and J.G.L. Puxton proceeded to BRAY to take up duties on the Light Railway under the C.E. 17th Corps. This party to be entirely rationed and administered by the 17th Corps. Two platoons of "C" Company under Lieut. J.M. Marshall proceeded to the village of NEUVILLE ST VAASTE for repairing front line trenches and communication trenches on the road from NEUVILLE ST VAASTE to the front line. This party is working under the 152nd Infantry Brigade. Two platoons of "C" Company under Captain G.W. Parkinson were posted to North of the village of LA TARGETTE on the BETHUNE-ARRAS Road for keeping communication trenches in repair and clear, and making new dugouts under the C.E. 17th Corps. "D" Company under Captain M. Montgomery proceeded to reserve line quarries, parapet B, North East of NEUVILLE-ST-VAASTE - PONTS and GOODMAN, and are engaged in making sections of five trenches connecting BOYEAU-FRANCE - PONTS and GOODMAN, and clearing an old trench communication trench under the C.R.E. 51st Division. The battalion Headquarters remained at LOUEZ.	

Army Form C. 2118.

WAR DIARY
or
INTELLIGENCE SUMMARY

(Erase heading not required.)

Place	Date	Hour	Summary of Events and Information	Remarks and references to Appendices
	June 28 1916 To June 30		All parties proceeded with the work allotted to them. Casualties June 21st to June 30th :- Sick 12. Total Strength June 30th :- 31 Officers 836 men.	

W.T.C. Westlake Lt Col
Commanding
12TH BN. LOYAL N. LANCS. REGT. (PIONEERS)

Army Form C. 2118.

WAR DIARY
or
INTELLIGENCE SUMMARY.
(Erase heading not required.)

Confidential.

War Diary

of

1/12th Bn. Loyal North Lancs. Regt. (Pioneers)

from 1st July 1916 to 31st July 1916

(Volume 2)

Army Form C. 2118.

WAR DIARY
or
INTELLIGENCE SUMMARY

(Erase heading not required.)

Instructions regarding War Diaries and Intelligence Summaries are contained in F. S. Regs., Part II. and the Staff Manual respectively. Title Pages will be prepared in manuscript.

Place	Date	Hour	Summary of Events and Information	Remarks and references to Appendices
	June 21		The battalion left SUTTON VENY CAMP, WARMINSTER, WILTSHIRE, in the early morning and embarked, less Transport, at SOUTHAMPTON, on the S.S. CESAREA, the Transport proceeding on the S.S. CITY OF DUNKIRK.	
	June 22		Landed at HAVRE 7 a.m. and proceeded to No I Rest Camp, POINT ST ADDRESSE. Landing Strength :- 31 Officers & 52 Other Ranks.	
	June 23		The battalion spent the day resting, with the exception of "C" Company who spent the afternoon from 4 to 7 pm keeping order in the V.D Camp and 50 men of "B" company who spend the night on guard at the V.D Camp. Left HAVRE 9 p.m.	
	June 24		Arrived ST POL 3 p.m. Detrained and marched to TERNAS where we were billeted for the night.	
	June 25		We rested at TERNAS all morning and left there at 3 p.m. and marched from there on the main ST. POL - ARRAS Road as far as HAUTE - AVESNES. From there, C and D Companies under Captain G. W. Parkinson proceeded to ACQ, and Headquarters with A and B Companies went on to LOUEZ where we arrived at 12-30 P.m. on the 26th, the Transport being left at DUISANS. Both the detachments at ACQ and LOUEZ were billeted.	
	June 26		The whole battalion remained all day at billets. We are attached to the 1/8th Bn. Royal Scots (Pioneers), 51st Highland Division, to take over their duties.	
	June 27		The battalion took up its working portions this evening. "A" Company under Captain J. P. Bayley went into Reserve Trenches at ARIANE to work on the defence of ENTONNOIR under	

WAR DIARY or INTELLIGENCE SUMMARY

Army Form C. 2118.

Place	Date	Hour	Summary of Events and Information	Remarks and references to Appendices
			The C.E. 17th Corps. One platoon of "B" Company under 2nd Lieut. J.E.S. Badger to ARIANE on "B" work under the C.R.E. 51st Division. One platoon of "B" Company under 2nd Lieut. R. Hodgkinson at LA MAISON BLANCHE for work on the FORK REDOUBT. The company and half mentioned are all on the ARRAS-BETHUNE ROAD between ECURIE and NEUVILLE ST. VAASTE. Two platoons of "B" Company made up to 120 men out of "A" company and under the command of Lieut. T.C.L. Farrar with Lieut. F. Barton-Smith and 2nd Lieuts. P.P. Button and J.G.L. Pinston proceeded to BRAY to take up duties on the Light Railway under the C.E. 17th Corps. This party to be entirely rationed and administered by the 17th Corps. Two platoons of "C" Company under Lieut. J.M. Marshall proceeded to the village of NEUVILLE ST VAASTE for repairing front line trenches and communication trenches on the road from NEUVILLE ST VAASTE to the front line. This party is working under the 152nd Infantry Brigade. Two platoons of "C" Company under Captain G.W. Parkinson were posted to North of the village of LA TARGETTE on the BETHUNE-ARRAS Road for keeping communication trenches in repair and clear, and making new dugouts under the C.E. 17th Corps. "D" company under Captain M. Montgomery proceeded to reserve line quarries, parapet 8, North East of NEUVILLE-ST-VAASTE and are engaged in making sections of fire trenches connecting BOYEAU-FRANCE-PONTS and GOODMAN, and clearing an old french communication trench under the C.R.E. 51st Division. The battalion Headquarters remained at LOUEZ.	

Army Form C. 2118.

WAR DIARY
or
INTELLIGENCE SUMMARY
(Erase heading not required.)

Place	Date	Hour	Summary of Events and Information	Remarks and references to Appendices
	1916 June 28 To June 30.		All parties proceeded with the work allotted to them. **Casualties** June 21st to June 30th :- **Sick** 12. **Total Strength** June 30th :- 31 Officers & 36 men.	

W.P.C. Berkeley Lt Col
Commanding
12TH BN. LOYAL N. LANCS. REGT. (PIONEERS)

Army Form C. 2118.

WAR DIARY
or
INTELLIGENCE SUMMARY.
(*Erase heading not required.*)

Instructions regarding War Diaries and Intelligence Summaries are contained in F.S. Regs., Part II. and the Staff Manual respectively. Title pages will be prepared in manuscript.

Hour, Date, Place	Summary of Events and Information	Remarks and references to Appendices
	Confidential. War Diary of 1/12th Bn. Royal North Lancs. Regt. (Pioneers) from 1st July 1916 to 31st July 1916 (Volume 2)	

Army Form C. 2118.

WAR DIARY
or
INTELLIGENCE SUMMARY.
(Erase heading not required.)

Instructions regarding War Diaries and Intelligence Summaries are contained in F.S. Regs., Part II and the Staff Manual respectively. Title pages will be prepared in manuscript.

Hour, Date, Place 1916	Summary of Events and Information	Remarks and references to Appendices
July 1st to 11th	Work proceeded at the points allotted to us as per the last entry in the War Diary for June.	
July 5th	One man of "D" Company was wounded at Reserve Line Quarries Parallel 8.	
July 12th	One man of "A" Company attached to 17th Corps Light Railway was wounded whilst taking up Rations at night.	
July 11th	The whole battalion were withdrawn from the trenches and concentrated at MAROEUIL, with the exception of Headquarters who remained at LOUEZ and two platoons of "B" Company employed on 17th Corps Light Railway. The battalion remained at MAROEUIL until July 13th.	
July 13th	when on the relief of the 51st Division we took over from the 1/8th Royal Scots (Pioneers) "D" Company proceeded to the Right Sector with two platoons at ECURIE and one platoon at ANZIN, and number 13 platoon under Lieut. Faulkner. S.H.D came to LOUEZ for 5 days rest. "A" Company proceeded to the Centre Sector at LA MAISON BLANCHE	

ns regarding War Diaries and Intelligence
Summaries are contained in F.S. Regs., Part II.
and the Staff Manual respectively. Title pages
will be prepared in manuscript.

WAR DIARY
or
INTELLIGENCE SUMMARY.
(Erase heading not required.)

Army Form C. 2118.

Hour, Date, Place	Summary of Events and Information	Remarks and references to Appendices
1916	on the BETHUNE-ARRAS ROAD. Number 7 platoon, "B" Company under 2nd Lieut R. Hodgkinson was attached to "A" Company until further Orders and remained behind at LOUEZ for rest. "C" Company, less number 10 platoon under 2nd Lieut C.T. Jackson, proceeded to the Left Sector at NEUVILLE-ST-VAASTE. Number 10 platoon remained at LOUEZ for rest. Number 8 platoon of "B" Company under 2nd Lieut J.E.S. Badger also remained at LOUEZ for rest. The work allotted to our companies in the trenches by the C.R.E. was, with the R.E. to work on the front line trenches, but them in a thorough state of repair and lowering the whole trench to a depth of 7 ft. All this work started on the night of the 13th. The Officers and men employed on the Light Railway remained on the Light Railway. The Commanding Officer, Lieut. Col. W.T.C. Beckett, V.D. established his Advance Headquarters at the Headquarters which had been occupied by the Officer Commanding 1/8 Royal Scots	

WAR DIARY
or
INTELLIGENCE SUMMARY.
(Erase heading not required.)

Army Form C. 2118.

Instructions regarding War Diaries and Intelligence Summaries are contained in F.S. Regs., Part II and the Staff Manual respectively. Title pages will be prepared in manuscript.

Hour, Date, Place	Summary of Events and Information	Remarks and references to Appendices
July 15th	at the point where the Annisoeure Trench crosses the BETHUNE-ARRAS ROAD.	
July 16th	Three men of "D" Company were wounded by shell fire in the Right Sector.	
	It was decided owing to the necessity of getting the work in the Front Line Trenches done quickly and the shortage of men in the Left Sector to send into the trenches to join "C" Company, number 10 platoon under 2nd Lieut. C.T. Jackson and number 8 platoon of "B" Company under 2nd Lieut. J.E.S. Botger. This latter platoon was attached to "C" Company from the 16th until further orders.	
	These platoons left for the trenches at 9 a.m.	
July 18th	A + D Companies' platoons at rest returned to the trenches and were replaced at LOVEZ by number 4 platoon of "A" Company under 2nd Lieut. J. Wood and number 14 platoon of "D" Company under Lieut. E D.M. Keyworth.	
July 23rd	The platoons at rest from "A" + "D" Companies returned to the trenches and were replaced at LOVEZ by No. 1 platoon	

Army Form C. 2118.

WAR DIARY
or
INTELLIGENCE SUMMARY.
(Erase heading not required.)

Instructions regarding War Diaries and Intelligence Summaries are contained in F.S. Regs., Part II. and the Staff Manual respectively. Title pages will be prepared in manuscript.

Hour, Date, Place	Summary of Events and Information	Remarks and references to Appendices
July 28th	"A" Company under Lieut. R.T. Powell, and no. 15 platoon of "D" Company under 2nd Lieut. P.P. Butler. The platoons at rest from "A" & "D" Companies returned to the trenches and were replaced at LOVEZ by no. 2 platoon of "A" Company under 2nd Lieut. F.M. Pawsey and no. 16 platoon of "D" Company under 2nd Lieut. H.E. Ward. "C" Company also sent in no. 12 platoon to rest under 2nd Lieut. J. Bowyer. Two men of "C" Company wounded in front of NEUVILLE-ST-VAASTE.	
July 30th	Casualties - July 1st to 31st. 3 Officers and 91 Other Ranks admitted to Hospital - Sick. 5 Other Ranks admitted to Hospital - Wounded. 2 Other Ranks admitted to Hospital - Accidentally Wounded. 3 Officers and 53 Other Ranks Returned to duty. 3 Other Ranks sent to England on leave. Total Strength - July 31st:- 31 Officers. 822 Other Ranks.	

Army Form C. 2118.

WAR DIARY
or
INTELLIGENCE SUMMARY.
(Erase heading not required.)

Instructions regarding War Diaries and Intelligence Summaries are contained in F.S. Regs., Part II. and the Staff Manual respectively. Title pages will be prepared in manuscript.

Hour, Date, Place	Summary of Events and Information	Remarks and references to Appendices
	The following promotions in the Battalion have been gazetted during the month.	
	"Extract from London Gazette dated 30th June 1916:-	
	2nd Lieut. (Temp. Lieut.) H. Wilkinson to be Temp. Captain. 30th June '16"	
	Extract from London Gazette dated 7th July 1916:-	
	Captain W. Longbottom to be Temp. Major. March 23rd 1916.	
	2nd Lieuts. (Temp. Lieuts.) J. Hatter and J.C.L. Furrow to be Temp. Captains. March 23rd 1916.	
	2nd Lieuts. S.H.C. Webster, C.D.M. Keyworth, A. Gillespie, R.T. Powell, S.N.D. Faulkner and J. White to be Temp. Lieuts.	
	2nd Lieut. (Temp. Captain) H. Wilkinson to be Adjutant, vice Captain (Temp. Major) W. Longbottom. July 9th 1916.	
	The following officers proceeded on Courses during the month:-	
	3rd Army Infantry School. Auxi le Chateau. Captain H. Wilkinson. Proceeded on 9th July 1916.	

Army Form C. 2118.

WAR DIARY
or
INTELLIGENCE SUMMARY.
(Erase heading not required.)

Instructions regarding War Diaries and Intelligence Summaries are contained in F.S. Regs., Part II. and the Staff Manual respectively. Title pages will be prepared in manuscript.

Hour, Date, Place	Summary of Events and Information	Remarks and references to Appendices
Transport Course with A.S.C. No 2 Camp. Havre.	2nd Lieut. S.H.D. Faulkner. Proceeded on 16th July 1916.	
Divisional Anti Gas School from Capelle.	July 15th to 18th 2nd Lieut. J.E.S. Rodger and 2 A.C. O's. July 19th to 21st 2nd Lt. and Lieut. G. Wood and 2 A.C. O's. July 22nd to 24th Lieut. C.D.M. Kaymouth and 2 A.C. O's. July 25th to 27th 2nd Lieut. PR Butter and 2 A.C. O's.	

Army Form C. 2118.

WAR DIARY
or
INTELLIGENCE SUMMARY.
(Erase heading not required.)

Instructions regarding War Diaries and Intelligence Summaries are contained in F.S. Regs., Part II. and the Staff Manual respectively. Title pages will be prepared in manuscript.

Date, 1916	Summary of Events and Information	Remarks and references to Appendices
July 1st to 11th	Work proceeded at the points allotted to us as per the last entry in the War Diary for June.	
July 5th	One man of "D" Company was wounded at Reserve Line Quarries Parallel 8.	
July 12th	One man of "A" Company attached to 17th Corps Light Railway was wounded whilst taking up Rations at night.	
July 11th	The whole battalion were withdrawn from the trenches and concentrated at MAROEUIL, with the exception of Headquarters who remained at LOUEZ and two platoons of "B" Company employed on 17th Corps Light Railway. The battalion remained at MAROEUIL until July 13th when on the relief of the 51st Division we took over from the 1/8th Royal Scots (Pioneers)	
July 13th	"D" Company proceeded to the Right Sector with two platoons at ECURIE and one platoon at ANZIN, and number 13 platoon under Lieut. Faulkner S.H.D. came to LOUEZ for 5 days rest. "A" Company proceeded to the Centre Sector at LA MAISON BLANCHE	

WAR DIARY
or
INTELLIGENCE SUMMARY.
(Erase heading not required.)

Army Form C. 2118.

Hour, Date, Place	Summary of Events and Information	Remarks and references to Appendices
1916	on the BETHUNE-ARRAS ROAD.	
	Number 7 Platoon, "B" Company under 2nd Lieut R. Hodgkinson was attached to "A" Company until further orders and remained behind at LOUEZ for rest.	
	"C" Company, less number 10 Platoon under 2nd Lieut C.T. Jackson, proceeded to the Left Sector at NEUVILLE-ST-VAASTE. Number 10 Platoon remained at LOUEZ for rest.	
	Number 8 Platoon of "B" Company under 2nd Lieut J.E.S. Badger also remained at LOUEZ for rest.	
	The work allotted to our companies in the trenches by the C.R.E. was, with the R.E. to work on the Front Line Trenches; but them in a thorough state of repair and lowering the whole trench to a depth of 7 ft. All this work started on the night of the 13th.	
	The Officers and men employed on the Light Railway remained on the Light Railway.	
	The Commanding Officer, Lieut. Col. W.T.C. Beckett. V.D. established his Advance Headquarters at the Headquarters which had been occupied by the Officer Commanding 1/8th Royal Scots	

WAR DIARY
or
INTELLIGENCE SUMMARY.

(Erase heading not required.)

Army Form C. 2118.

Hour, Date, Place	Summary of Events and Information	Remarks and references to Appendices
	at the point where the Annequin Trench crosses the BETHUNE-ARRAS ROAD.	
July 15th	Three men of "D" Company were wounded by shell fire in the Right Sector.	
July 16th	It was decided owing to the necessity of getting the work in the Front Line Trenches done quickly and the shortage of men in the Left Sector to send into the trenches to join "C" Company. number 10 platoon under 2nd Lieut. C.T. Jackson and number 8 platoon of "B" Company under 2nd Lieut. J.S. Badger. The latter platoon was attached to "C" Company from the 16th until further orders. These platoons left for the trenches at 9 a.m.	
July 18th	A & D Companies' platoons at rest returned to the trenches and were replaced at LOUEZ by number 4 platoon of "A" Company under 2nd Lieut. J. Wood and number 14 platoon of "D" Company under Lieut. C.D.M. Keyworth.	
July 23rd	The platoons at rest from "A" & "D" Companies returned to the trenches and were replaced at LOUEZ by No. 2 platoon	

WAR DIARY
or
INTELLIGENCE SUMMARY.
(Erase heading not required.)

Army Form C. 2118.

Hour, Date, Place	Summary of Events and Information	Remarks and references to Appendices
July 28th	¶ "A" Company under Lieut. R.T. Powell, and No. 15 platoon of "D" Company under 2nd Lieut. P.P. Butters. The platoons at rest from "A" & "D" Companies returned to the trenches and were replaced at LOVEZ by No. 2 platoon of "A" Company under 2nd Lieut. A.M. Pantry and No. 16 platoon of "D" Company under 2nd Lieut. N.B. Hazel. "C" Company also sent in No. 12 platoon to rest under 2nd Lieut. G. Boyer.	
July 30th	Two men of "C" Company wounded in front of NEUVILLE-ST-VAASTE. Casualties :- July 1st to 31st 3 Officers and 91 Other Ranks admitted to Hospital - Sick. 5 Other Ranks admitted to Hospital - Wounded 2 Other Ranks admitted to Hospital - Accidentally Wounded. 3 Officers and 53 Other Ranks Returned to duty. 3 Other Ranks sent to England under age. Total Strength - July 31st :- 31 Officers 822 Other Ranks.	

Army Form C. 2118.

WAR DIARY
or
INTELLIGENCE SUMMARY.
(Erase heading not required.)

Hour, Date, Place	Summary of Events and Information	Remarks and references to Appendices
	The following promotions in the Battalion have been gazetted during the month.-	
	"Extract from London gazette dated 30th June 1916.-	
	2nd Lieut. (Temp. Lieut) H. Wilkinson to be Temp. Captain. 30 June 16"	
	Extract from London gazette dated 7th July 1916.- Captain W. Longbottom to be Temp. Major. March 23rd 1916. 2nd Lieuts. (Temp. Lieuts.) J. Watters and J.C.L. Farrar to be Temp. Captains. March 23rd 1916.	
	2nd Lieuts. S.H.C. Webster, C.D.M. Keyworth, A. Gillespie, R.T. Powell, S.H.D. Faulkner and J. White to be Temp. Lieuts.	
	2nd Lieut. (Temp. Captain) H. Wilkinson to be Adjutant, vice Captain (Temp. Major) W. Longbottom. July 9th 1916.	
	The following officers proceeded on courses during the month:-	
	3rd Army Infantry School, Auxi-le-Chateau. Captain H. Wilkinson. Proceeded on 9th July 1916.	

Army Form C. 2118.

WAR DIARY
or
INTELLIGENCE SUMMARY.
(Erase heading not required.)

Instructions regarding War Diaries and Intelligence Summaries are contained in F.S. Regs., Part II. and the Staff Manual respectively. Title pages will be prepared in manuscript.

Hour, Date, Place	Summary of Events and Information	Remarks and references to Appendices
	Transport Course with A.S.C. No 2 Camp. Havre.	2nd Lieut. S.N.D. Faulkner Proceeded on 16th July 1916.
	Divisional Anti Gas School Frein Capelle:	July 15th to 18th 2nd Lieut J.E.S. Bodget and 2 N.C.O's.
		July 19th to 21st 2nd Lieut. G. Wood and 2 N.C.O's
		July 22nd to 24th Lieut. C.D.M. Keyworth and 2 N.C.O's
		July 25th to 27th 2nd Lieut. P.P. Butter and 2 N.C.O's.

Army Form C. 2118.

WAR DIARY
or
INTELLIGENCE SUMMARY.
(Erase heading not required.)

Vol III

Confidential.

War Diary

of

1/12th Bn. Loyal North Lancs. Regt. (Pioneers)

August 1st 1916 to August 31st 1916.

(Volume 3.)

Army Form C. 2118.

WAR DIARY
or
INTELLIGENCE SUMMARY.
(Erase heading not required.)

Hour, Date, Place	Summary of Events and Information	Remarks and references to Appendices
August 1st	Lieut. J. Barton-Smith transferred from "B" Company on 17th Corps Light Railway to "A" Company as 2nd in Command. Lieut. S. H. C. Webster transferred from in charge of Lewis Gun Section to "B" Company on 17th Corps Light Railway. 2nd Lieut. C. T. Jackson came in from "C" Company to take charge of Lewis Gun Section.	
2nd	The platoons of "A", "C" and "D" Companies at rest returned to the trenches and were replaced at LOUEZ by No. 7 Platoon of "B" Company attached to "A" Company under 2nd Lieut. R. Hodgkinson, No. 11 Platoon of "C" Company under 2nd Lieut. B. Moore and No. 13 Platoon of "D" Company under 2nd Lieut. L. A. Cooke. 2nd Lieut. L. A. Cooke was transferred today from "C" Company to "D" Company.	
3rd	One man was severely wounded by a sniper in front line trenches in Centre Sector whilst making a Trench Mortar emplacement.	

WAR DIARY
or
INTELLIGENCE SUMMARY.

(Erase heading not required.)

Army Form C. 2118.

Instructions regarding War Diaries and Intelligence Summaries are contained in F.S. Regs., Part II. and the Staff Manual respectively. Title pages will be prepared in manuscript.

Hour, Date, Place	Summary of Events and Information	Remarks and references to Appendices
August 5th	Captain H. Wilkinson returned from 3rd Army Infantry School and took up his duties as Adjutant. Received gas alarm at 4.3 p.m. All stood to until cancelled at 5.42 p.m. Time taken to stand to 15 minutes.	
7th	The Platoons of "A", "C" and "D" Companies at rest returned to the trenches and were replaced at LOUEZ by No. 4 Platoon of "A" Company under 2nd Lieut. G. Wood, No. 9 Platoon of "C" Company and No. 14 Platoon of "D" Company.	
8th	Received gas alarm at 10-30 p.m. All stood to until cancelled. Time taken to stand to 10 minutes. Ten Officers as under reported for duty at LOUEZ from the Reserve Battalion at OSWESTRY. Captain J. M. Turnbull. 2nd Lieut. R. W. Williams. 2nd Lieut. S. M. Bradbury. 2nd Lieut. G. M. McCorquodale. 2nd Lieut. W. F. Hedges. 2nd Lieut. C. A. Young. 2nd Lieut. J. J. Tucker. 2nd Lieut. N. R. C. Chase. 2nd Lieut. E. H. Treacy. 2nd Lieut. E. J. Hart.	
10th	Captain J. M. Turnbull appointed Town Major of LOUEZ. 2nd Lieut. G. M. McCorquodale and 2nd Lieut. E. J. Hart proceeded to duty with "A" Company in the trenches at LA MAISON BLANCHE.	

WAR DIARY
or
INTELLIGENCE SUMMARY.
(Erase heading not required.)

Army Form C. 2118.

Instructions regarding War Diaries and Intelligence Summaries are contained in F.S. Regs., Part II. and the Staff Manual respectively. Title pages will be prepared in manuscript.

Hour, Date, Place	Summary of Events and Information	Remarks and references to Appendices
August 10th	2nd Lieut. C.A. Young proceeded to duty with "B" Company's platoon attached to "C" Company at NEUVILLE ST VAASTE. 2nd Lieut. J.J. Tinkwit and 2nd Lieut. H.N.C. Chase proceeded to duty with "C" Company in the trenches at NEUVILLE ST VAASTE. 2nd Lieut. R.N. Williams proceeded to duty with "D" Company in the trenches at ECURIE. 2nd Lieut. Tracey, 2nd Lieut. Bradbury and 2nd Lieut. Hedges remained at LOVEZ and took over the Platoons of "A", "C" and "D" Companies at rest.	
August 11th	One man killed by piece of shell in front line trenches in left Sector. – P/612 Cpl. Sawbury, 7.A. "C" Company.	
12th	The Platoons of "A", "C" and "D" Companies returned to the trenches and were replaced at LOVEZ by No. 1 Platoon of "A" Company under Lieut. Powell, No. 3 Platoon of "B" Company attached to "C" Company under 2nd Lieut. J.E.S. Badger and 2nd Lieut. C.A. Young. No. 10 Platoon of "C" Company under Lieut. A. Gillespie and No. 13 Platoon of "D" Company under 2nd Lieut. T.P. Buttery. Lieut. & H.D. Faulknor reported from Transport Course at HAVRE. Service by Rev. Patten.	Report on Lieut Jenkins's court very satisfactory

One Sawbury buried in Cemetery at LOVEZ.

WAR DIARY
or
INTELLIGENCE SUMMARY.
(Erase heading not required.)

Army Form C. 2118.

Hour, Date, Place	Summary of Events and Information	Remarks and references to Appendices
August 14th	P.782 Pte J. Dean and P.1514 Pte Huyton. J. tried by Field General Court Martial on charge of Absence without leave from 2 p.m. 4/8/16 to 6 p.m. 6/8/1916.	
15th	Lieut S.H.D. Faulkner appointed Transport Officer vice Lieut J. White to remain as assistant.	
16th	Sentence on P.782 Pte J. Dean – 35 days Field Punishment no.1 Sentence on P.1514 Pte J. Huyton – 28 days Field Punishment no.1 Promulgated 11 A.M. today.	
17th	Captain N.P. Laing, R.A.M.C., Medical Officer was admitted to Field Ambulance – sick. Captain L.L. Thornton, R.A.M.C. 2/6th London Field Ambulance reported for duty as temporary Medical Officer. The Platoons of "B","C","D" Companies returned to the trenches and were replaced at LOVEZ by no 2 Platoon of "A" Company under 2nd Lieut. A.M. Parvey and 2nd Lieut. E.J. Hart, No 12 Platoon of "C" Company under 2nd Lieut. J. Boyer and No 16 Platoon of "D" Company under 2nd Lieut. H.E. Ward.	

WAR DIARY
or
INTELLIGENCE SUMMARY.
(Erase heading not required.)

Army Form C. 2118.

Instructions regarding War Diaries and Intelligence Summaries are contained in F.S. Regs., Part II and the Staff Manual respectively. Title pages will be prepared in manuscript.

Hour, Date, Place	Summary of Events and Information	Remarks and references to Appendices
August 17	Captain Bayley O.C "A" Company reported at Headquarters LOVEZ, sick.	
18	Commenced an afternoon Wiring Class under R.E Instructor for Platoons at rest.	
19	Major W. Longbottom left LOVEZ to take temporary command of "D" Company at ECURIE, to enable Captain Montgomery to devote his time to Defence Scheme. Disbanded old (permanent) guard and commenced taking guards from Platoons at rest.	
20	Commanding Officer came in to LOVEZ from ARIANE for rest. Major A. Buckley went out to ARIANE from LOVEZ to take over duty. Lieut Pettifer A.P.H came in to LOVEZ from ARIANE for rest.	
21	Received Gas Alarm at 11-15 p.m. Cancelled at 11-25 p.m. Signal given to take cover from aeroplane, quickly followed by all clear. Splinter proof shell brought down telephone wires which were quickly repaired.	

Army Form C. 2118.

WAR DIARY
or
INTELLIGENCE SUMMARY.
(Erase heading not required.)

Hour, Date, Place	Summary of Events and Information	Remarks and references to Appendices
August 22nd	2nd Lieut. J. Boyes, 1 N.C.O and 6 men of "C" Company left LOUEZ at 2/pm for special work in the trenches. The Platoons of A, C & D Companies at rest returned to the trenches and were replaced at LOUEZ by No 7 Platoon of "B" Company attached to "A" Company under 2nd Lieut R. Hodgkinson and 2nd Lieut. P.P. Button, No. 11 Platoon of "C" Company under 2nd Lieut B. Moore and 2nd Lieut J.J. Tinker and No 13 Platoon of "D" Company under 2nd Lieut. L.A. Corke. P.632 Cpl. E. Ashurst tried by Field General Court Martial charged with (1) Drunk in Reserve Area and (ii) Absent without leave from 5/pm 16/8/16 to 2/pm 16/8/16. P.745 Pte. P. Hutchinson tried by Field General Court Martial charged with being drunk when on duty in Reserve Area.	
24th	Sentence on P.632 Cpl. E. Ashurst - Reduced to Ranks and 30 days Field Punishment No 1 Sentence on P.745 Pte P. Hutchinson - Fined 10/-3 and 60 days Field Punishment No 2. Promulgated 11 A.M. today.	

Army Form C. 2118.

WAR DIARY
or
INTELLIGENCE SUMMARY.
(Erase heading not required.)

Instructions regarding War Diaries and Intelligence Summaries are contained in F.S. Regs., Part II and the Staff Manual respectively. Title pages will be prepared in manuscript.

Hour, Date, Place	Summary of Events and Information	Remarks and references to Appendices
August 23rd	Captain M. Montgomery "D" Company and Captain J.M. Marshall	
24th	"C" Company came in to LOVEZ for rest. Barn opposite Headquarters Chateau at LOVEZ caught fire at 11-30 a.m. and was gutted. Fire piquet confined the fire to building in which it started.	
27th	The platoons of A.C. and D Companies at rest returned to the trenches and were replaced at LOVEZ by No. 4 platoon of "A" Company under 2nd Lieut. G. Wood and 2nd Lieut. E.H. Treacy, No 9 platoon of "C" Company under 2nd Lieut. S.M. Bradbury and No 14 platoon of "D" Company under 2nd Lieut. L.A. Cooke. Two men wounded whilst working on the 17th Corps Light Railway. Captain J.M. Marshall "C" Company returned to duty in the trenches tonight.	
28th		
30th	The platoons at rest and Lewis Gun Section worked all day at Transport lines preparing Winter Standings for horses. Two men wounded (shell shock) in front line trenches at NEUVILLE ST VAASTE.	

WAR DIARY
or
INTELLIGENCE SUMMARY.
(Erase heading not required.)

Army Form C. 2118.

Hour, Date, Place	Summary of Events and Information	Remarks and references to Appendices
August 31st	No. 22,280 2/Cpl. D. Reaside 2/3rd Royal Dublin Fusiliers attached to this Battalion was tried by Field General Court Martial charged with being drunk on Active Service. Lieut. R.T. Powell Returned to the trenches tonight. Casualties - August 1st to 31st 2 Officers and 73 Other Ranks admitted to Hospital - Sick. 5 Other Ranks admitted to Hospital - Wounded. 1 Other Rank - Killed. 1 Other Rank - Died of Wounds 3 Other Ranks sent to Base for Dental Treatment. 1 Other Rank sent to Base - Under age 1 Officer and 44 Other Ranks returned to duty. Total Strength - August 31st 40 Officers 788 Other Ranks.	

Army Form C. 2118.

WAR DIARY
or
INTELLIGENCE SUMMARY.
(Erase heading not required.)

Instructions regarding War Diaries and Intelligence Summaries are contained in F. S. Regs., Part II. and the Staff Manual respectively. Title pages will be prepared in manuscript.

Hour, Date, Place	Summary of Events and Information	Remarks and references to Appendices
	The following promotions in the Battalion have been gazetted during the month.	
	Extract from London Gazette of 14th August 1916:-	
	2nd Lieut (Temp. Lieut) J. M. Marshall to be Temp. Captain June 21st 1916.	
	2nd Lieut P. H. Pettiford to be Temporary Lieut June 21st 1916.	
	2nd Lieut J. E. S. Rodger to be Temporary Lieut. June 30th 1916.	
	The following Officers proceeded on Courses during the month :-	
	3rd Army Infantry School. Auxi-le-Chateau.	Captain T. Watters proceeded on 8th August 1916.
	Divisional Anti-Gas School. Ferrin Capelle.	July 31st to Aug 2nd 2nd Lieut. E. Bryan and 2 N.C.O's.
		Aug 3rd to Aug 5th 2nd Lieut. R. Hodgkinson and 2 N.C.O's.
	Lewis Gun Course LA TOUQUET	Lieut. R. T. Powell proceeded on 31st August 1916. returned on 30th August 1916.

Army Form C. 2118.

WAR DIARY
or
INTELLIGENCE SUMMARY.
(Erase heading not required.)

Instructions regarding War Diaries and Intelligence Summaries are contained in F.S. Regs., Part II. and the Staff Manual respectively. Title pages will be prepared in manuscript.

Hour, Date, Place	Summary of Events and Information	Remarks and references to Appendices
	Summary of Work done from June to August 31st 1916.	
	747 Sumps Completed.	
	13,062 feet Duckboards laid.	
	7 Dug outs made and completed.	
	1,445 sqr. yds of Trench Sand-bag revetted	
	5,615 yards of trench deepened to 7 feet.	
	2,615 yards of trench drained	
	826 yards of trench Revetted.	
	1,229 yards of pipe trench dug.	
	45 Traverses and Fire bays erected.	
	4 Fire Posts erected.	
	1 Crater being consolidated (Pulpit)	
	2 Snipers Posts erected. 1 on Tidza Crater. 1 on Chassery Crater.	
	2 Trench Mortar Emplacements erected.	
	1 Machine Gun Emplacement erected	
	1 Water Tank Emplacement erected.	
	197 Frames made for Emplacements.	
	Besides other numerous minor works Completed.	
	Work in Progress.	
	5 Dug outs in Progress.	
	1 Trench Mortar Emplacement in Progress, and Crater Consolidation.	

Army Form C. 2118.

WAR DIARY
or
INTELLIGENCE SUMMARY.
(Erase heading not required.)

Hour, Date, Place	Summary of Events and Information	Remarks and references to Appendices
	Confidential War Diary of 1/12th Bn. Loyal North Lancs. Regt. (Pioneers) August 1st 1916 to August 31st 1916. (Volume 3.)	

Instructions regarding War Diaries and Intelligence Summaries are contained in F.S. Regs., Part II. and the Staff Manual respectively. Title pages will be prepared in manuscript.

WAR DIARY
or
INTELLIGENCE SUMMARY.
(Erase heading not required.)

Army Form C. 2118.

Hour, Date, Place	Summary of Events and Information	Remarks and references to Appendices
August 1st	Lieut. J. Barton-Smith transferred from "B" Company on 17th Corps Light Railway to "A" Company as 2nd in Command. Lieut. S. H. C. Webster transferred from in charge of Lewis Gun Section to "B" Company on 17th Corps Light Railway. 2nd Lieut. C. T. Jackson came in from "C" Company to take charge of Lewis Gun Section.	
2nd	The platoons of "A", "C" and "D" Companies at rest returned to the trenches and were replaced at LOUEZ by No. 7 platoon of "B" Company attached to "A" Company under 2nd Lieut. R. Hodgkinson, No. 11 platoon of "C" Company under 2nd Lieut. B. Moore and No. 13 platoon of "D" Company under 2nd Lieut. R. A. Cooke. 2nd Lieut. R. A. Cooke was transferred today from "C" Company to "D" Company.	
3rd	One man was severely wounded by a sniper in front line trenches in Centre Sector whilst making a Trench Mortar emplacement.	

WAR DIARY
or
INTELLIGENCE SUMMARY.
(Erase heading not required.)

Army Form C. 2118.

Hour, Date, Place	Summary of Events and Information	Remarks and references to Appendices
August 5th	Captain A. Wilkinson returned from 3rd Army Infantry School and took up his duties as Adjutant. Received gas alarm at 4.3 pm. All stood to until cancelled at 5.42 pm. Time taken to stand to - 15 minutes.	
7th	The platoons of "A", "C" and "D" Companies at rest returned to the trenches and were replaced at LOUEZ by No.4 Platoon of "A" Company under 2nd Lieut G. Wood, No. 9 Platoon of "C" Company and No. 14 Platoon of "D" Company.	
8th	Received gas alarm at 10-30 pm. All stood to until cancelled. Ten Officers as under reported for duty at LOUEZ from the Reserve Battalion at OSWESTRY. Captain J. M. Turnbull. 2nd Lieut C. A. Young 2nd Lieut R.W. Williams. 2nd Lieut J. J. Tucker 2nd Lieut S. M. Bradbury 2nd Lieut H. N. C. Chase 2nd Lieut G. M. McCorquodale 2nd Lieut E. H. Tracy 2nd Lieut H. T. Hedges. 2nd Lieut. E. J. Hart.	
10th	Captain J. M. Turnbull appointed Town Major of LOUEZ. 2nd Lieut G. M. McCorquodale and 2nd Lieut E. J. Hart proceeded to duty with "A" Company in the trenches at LA MAISON BLANCHE.	

Army Form C. 2118.

WAR DIARY
or
INTELLIGENCE SUMMARY.
(Erase heading not required.)

Instructions regarding War Diaries and Intelligence Summaries are contained in F.S. Regs., Part II. and the Staff Manual respectively. Title pages will be prepared in manuscript.

Hour, Date, Place	Summary of Events and Information	Remarks and references to Appendices
August 10th	2nd Lieut. C. A. Young proceeded to duty with "B" Company; Platoons attached to "C" Company at NEUVILLE ST VAASTE.	
	2nd Lieut. J. J. Tucker and 2nd Lieut. H. N. C. Chase proceeded to duty with "C" Company in the trenches at NEUVILLE ST VAASTE.	
	2nd Lieut. R. W. Williams proceeded to duty with "D" Company in the trenches at ECURIE.	
	2nd Lieut. Treacy, 2nd Lieut. Bradbury and 2nd Lieut. Hodges remained at LOUEZ and took over the Platoons of "A","C" and "D" Companies at rest.	
	One man killed by piece of Shell in front line trenches in left Sector. - P. 642 Cpl. Rawlinsey J.H. "C" Company.	
August 11th	The Platoons of "A","C" and "D" Companies returned to the trenches and were replaced at LOUEZ by No 1 Platoon of "A" Company under Lieut Powell, No. 8 Platoon of "B" Company, attached to "C" Company under 2nd Lieut J. S. Badger and 2nd Lieut. C. A. Young, No 10 Platoon of "C" Company under Lieut. A. Gillespie and No 15 platoon of "D" Company under 2nd Lieut. P. P. Butters.	
12th	Lieut. & S. H. D. Faulkner reported from Transport Course at HAVRE. Cpl Bradley buried in Cemetery at LOUEZ. Service by Rev. Patten.	Report on Lieut Faulkner course very satisfactory.

WAR DIARY
or
INTELLIGENCE SUMMARY.
(Erase heading not required.)

Army Form C. 2118.

Hour, Date, Place	Summary of Events and Information	Remarks and references to Appendices
August 14th	P.782 Pte J. Dean and P.1514 Pte Huyton. J. tried by Field General Court Martial on charge of Absence without leave from 2 pm 4/8/16 to 6 pm 6/8/1916.	
15th	Lieut S.H.D. Faulkner appointed Transport Officer vice Lieut J. White to remain as assistant.	
16th	Sentence on P.782 Pte J. Dean – 35 days Field Punishment No 1 Sentence on P.1514 Pte J. Huyton – 28 days Field Punishment No 1 Promulgated 11 A.M. today.	
17th	Captain N.P. Leung. R.A.M.C. Medical Officer was admitted to Field Ambulance – sick. Captain J.L. Thornton. R.A.M.C. 2/6th London Field Ambulance reported for duty as temporary Medical Officer. The Platoons of "A" "B" "C" "D" Companies returned to the trenches and were replaced at LOVEZ by no 2 Platoon of "A" Company under 2nd Lieut. A.M. Parry and 2nd Lieut. E.J. Hart; No 12 Platoon of "C" Company under 2nd Lieut. J. Boyers and No 16 Platoon of "D" Company under 2nd Lieut. H.E. Ward.	

Army Form C. 2118.

WAR DIARY
or
INTELLIGENCE SUMMARY.
(Erase heading not required.)

Instructions regarding War Diaries and Intelligence Summaries are contained in F.S. Regs., Part II. and the Staff Manual respectively. Title pages will be prepared in manuscript.

Hour, Date, Place	Summary of Events and Information	Remarks and references to Appendices
August 17 LOUEZ	Captain Bayley O.C "A" Company reported at Headquarters sick.	
18	Commenced an afternoon Wiring Class under R.E Instructor for platoons at rest.	
19	Major W. Longbottom left LOUEZ to take temporary command of "D" Company at ECURIE, to enable Captain Montgomery to devote his time to Defence Scheme. Disbanded old (permanent) guard and commenced taking guards from platoons at rest.	
20	Commanding Officer came in to LOUEZ from ARIANE for rest. Major A. Buckley went out to ARIANE from LOUEZ to take over duty. Lieut. Pettiford P.H. came in to LOUEZ from ARIANE for rest. Received gas alarm at 11-15 p.m. Cancelled at 11-25 p.m.	
21	Signal given to take cover from aeroplane, quickly followed by all clear. Splinter of shell brought down telephone wire which was quickly repaired.	

(73989) W4141—463. 400,000. 9/14. H.&J.Ltd. Forms/C. 2118/10.

WAR DIARY
or
INTELLIGENCE SUMMARY.
(Erase heading not required.)

Army Form C. 2118.

Hour, Date, Place	Summary of Events and Information	Remarks and references to Appendices
August 22nd	2nd Lieut. G. Boyer, 1 N.C.O and 6 men of "C" Company left LOUEZ at 2 pm for special work in the trenches. The platoons of A, C & D Companies at rest returned to the trenches and were replaced at LOUEZ by No 7 Platoon of "B" Company attached to "A" Company under 2nd Lieut. R. Hodgkinson and 2nd Lieut. P.P. Butler, No. 11 platoon of "C" Company under 2nd Lieut B. Moore and 2nd Lieut J.J. Tinker and No 13 platoon of "D" Company under 2nd Lieut. L. A. Corke. P.632 Cpl. E. Ashurst tried by Field General Court Martial charged with (1) Drunk in Reserve Area and (11) Absent without leave from 5 pm 16/8/16 to 8 pm. 16/8/16. P.745 Pte P. Hutchinson tried by Field General Court Martial charged with being drunk when on duty in Reserve Area.	
24th	Sentence on P.632 Cpl. E. Ashurst – Reduced to Ranks and 30 days Field Punishment No 1. Sentence on P.745 Pte P. Hutchinson – Fined 10/- and 60 days Field Punishment No I. Promulgated 11 A.M. today.	

Army Form C. 2118.

WAR DIARY
or
INTELLIGENCE SUMMARY.
(Erase heading not required.)

Instructions regarding War Diaries and Intelligence Summaries are contained in F.S. Regs., Part II. and the Staff Manual respectively. Title pages will be prepared in manuscript.

Hour, Date, Place	Summary of Events and Information	Remarks and references to Appendices
August 23rd	Captain M. Montgomery "D" Company and Captain J. M. Marshall "C" Company came in to LOUEZ for rest.	
24th	Barn opposite Headquarters Chateau at LOUEZ caught fire at 11-30 a.m. and was gutted. Fire picquet confined the fire to building in which it started.	
27th	The platoons of A.C. and D Companies at rest returned to the trenches and were replaced at LOUEZ by No. 4 platoon of "A" Company under 2nd Lieut. G. Wood and 2nd Lieut. E. H. Treacy, No. 9 platoon of "C" Company under 2nd Lieut. S. M. Bradbury and No. 14 platoon of "D" Company under 2nd Lieut. L. A. Cooke. Two men wounded whilst working on the 17th Corps Light Railway. Captain J. M. Marshall "C" Company returned to duty in the trenches tonight.	
28th		
30th	The platoons at rest and Lewis Gun Section worked all day at Transport lines preparing Winter Standings for horses. Two men wounded (shell shock) in front line trenches at NEUVILLE ST VAASTE.	

WAR DIARY
or
INTELLIGENCE SUMMARY.
(Erase heading not required.)

Army Form C. 2118.

Hour, Date, Place	Summary of Events and Information	Remarks and references to Appendices
August 31st	No. 22280 L/Cpl D. Reaside 2/5th Royal Dublin Fusiliers attached to this Battalion was tried by Field General Court Martial charged with being drunk on Active Service. Lieut. R.T. Powell returned to trenches tonight. Casualties - August 1st to 31st 2 Officers and 73 Other Ranks admitted to Hospital - Sick. 5 Other Ranks admitted to Hospital - Wounded. 1 Other Rank - Killed. 1 Other Rank - Died of Wounds 3 Other Ranks sent to Base for Dental Treatment. 1 Other Rank sent to Base - Under age 1 Officer and 44 Other Ranks returned to Duty. Total Strength - August 31st 40 Officers 788 Other Ranks.	

Army Form C. 2118.

WAR DIARY
or
INTELLIGENCE SUMMARY.
(Erase heading not required.)

Hour, Date, Place	Summary of Events and Information	Remarks and references to Appendices
Lewis Gun Course LA TOUQUET.	The following promotions in the Battalion have been gazetted during the month. Extract from London Gazette of 17th August 1916:- 2nd Lieut (Temp. Lieut) J. M. Marshall to be Temp. Captain June 21st 1916. 2nd Lieut. P. H. Pettiford to be Temporary Lieut June 21st 1916. 2nd Lieut J. E. S. Badger to be Temporary Lieut. June 30th 1916. The following Officers proceeded on Courses during the month :- 3rd Army Infantry School. Captain T. Watters Auxi-le-Chateau. proceeded on 8th August 1916. Divisional Anti Gas School. July 31st to Aug 2nd 2nd Lieut. G. Boyer and 2 N.C.O's. Huron Capelle. Aug 3rd to Aug 5th 2nd Lieut. R. Hodgkinson and 2 N.C.O's. Lieut. R. T. Powell proceeded on 21st August 1916. returned on 30th August 1916	

WAR DIARY
or
INTELLIGENCE SUMMARY.
(Erase heading not required.)

Army Form C. 2118.

Hour, Date, Place	Summary of Events and Information	Remarks and references to Appendices
	Summary of Work done from June to August 31st 1916.	

747 Sumps Completed.
13,062 feet Duckboards laid.
7 Dug outs made and completed.
1,445 sap yds of Trench Sand bag revetted.
5,615 yards of trench deepened to 7 feet.
2,615 yards of trench drained.
826 yards of trench Revetted.
1,229 yards of pipe trench dug.
45 Traverses and Fire bays erected.
4 Fire Posts erected.
1 Crater being consolidated (Pulpit)
2 Snipers Posts erected. 1 on Tidga Crater. 1 on Chancery Crater.
2 Trench Mortar Emplacements erected.
1 Machine gun Emplacement erected.
1 Water Tank Emplacement erected.
197 Frames made for Emplacements.
Besides other numerous minor works Completed.

Work In Progress.

5 Dug outs in Progress.
1 Trench Mortar Emplacement in Progress and Crater Consolidation

Army Form C. 2118.

WAR DIARY
or
INTELLIGENCE SUMMARY.
(Erase heading not required.)

Confidential

War Diary
of
1/12th Bn. Royal North Lancs. Regt. (Pioneer)

from 1st September to 30th September 1916.

(Volume 4)

Vol 4

Army Form C. 2118.

WAR DIARY
or
INTELLIGENCE SUMMARY.

(Erase heading not required.)

Instructions regarding War Diaries and Intelligence Summaries are contained in F.S. Regs., Part II and the Staff Manual respectively. Title pages will be prepared in manuscript.

Hour, Date, Place	Summary of Events and Information	Remarks and references to Appendices
1916. September 1st.	2/Lieuts. H.S. Lewis and H.P. Muckleston reported for duty at LOUEZ from the Reserve Battalion at Oswestry. 3 men reported for duty from a Cold Shoeing Course and were sent to the Transport Lines.	
3rd.	2/Lieuts. H.S. Lewis and H.P. Muckleston were posted to "D" Company and proceeded to duty in the Trenches at ECURIE. The platoons of "A", "C" and "D" Companies at rest returned to the Trenches and were replaced at LOUEZ by No. 1 platoon of "A" Company under 2nd Lieut. G.M. McCorquodale, No. 8 platoon of "B" Company attached to "C" Company, under Lieut. J.E.S. Bodger and 2nd Lieut. C.A. Young, No. 10 platoon of "C" Company under Lieut. A. Gillespie and No. 15 platoon of "D" Company under 2nd Lieut. W.F. Hedges. Sentence on No. 22,280 L/Cpl. D. Reaside, 2/3rd Royal Dublin Fusilier. 6 months Hard Labour. Commuted to 2 months Field Punishment No. 1. Promulgated at 11.15 a.m. to-day. *Lieut F Barton-Smith came out to rest.*	
4th.	Lieut. R.T. Powell, "A" Company came out from the Trenches to-day for rest.	
6th	Major W. Longbottom came in to LOUEZ from "D" company for rest. 2nd Lieut. H.E. Ward proceeded with 17 men and servant on Lewis Gun Course at Le Touquet, Etaples. No. 3686 R.S.M. Connor M.C. left LOUEZ to report to No. 25 Infantry	

Army Form C. 2118.

WAR DIARY
or
INTELLIGENCE SUMMARY.
(Erase heading not required.)

Instructions regarding War Diaries and Intelligence Summaries are contained in F.S. Regs., Part II. and the Staff Manual respectively. Title pages will be prepared in manuscript.

Hour, Date, Place	Summary of Events and Information	Remarks and references to Appendices
September 6th (Contd)	Base Depot, ETAPLES.	
8th	Lieut. F. Barton-Smith "A" Company returned to duty in the Trenches.	
9th	No. P.70 Pte. W. Kenyon was tried by F.G.C.M. on a charge of "Using insubordinate language to his superior officer".	
	Two men of this battalion were detailed to assist local farmer with Harvesting.	
10th.	2nd Lieut. S.H. Bailey was sent to the Transport Lines to assist Lieut. J. White during the absence of Lieut. S.H.D. Faulkner, - sick.	
	The platoons of "A", "B", "C" and "D" companies at rest returned to duty in the trenches.	
	Platoons out for rest :-	
	"A" Company No. 2 Platoon under 2nd Lieut. E.J. Hart.	
	"C" Company No 12 Platoon under 2nd Lieuts. G. Bryers and H.N.C. Chase.	
	"D" Company No 16 Platoon under 2nd Lieut. H.S. Lewis.	
	Major W. Longbotton came in to LOUEZ from ARIANE and proceeded to Hospital suffering from P.U.O.	
11th	Sentence on No. P.70 Pte. W. Kenyon - 12 months Hard Labour. Promulgated to-day.	
	1 Officer and 32 men of No. 15 Plat.on "D" Company and 1 Officer and 24 men of No. 4 Platoon "A" Company proceeded to LA TARGETTE under 2nd Lieut. B. Moore.	

Army Form C. 2118.

WAR DIARY
or
INTELLIGENCE SUMMARY.
(Erase heading not required.)

Instructions regarding War Diaries and Intelligence Summaries are contained in F.S. Regs., Part II. and the Staff Manual respectively. Title pages will be prepared in manuscript.

Hour, Date, Place	Summary of Events and Information	Remarks and references to Appendices
September 12th.	Major W. Longbottom returned to LOUEZ from Hospital. 2nd Lieut. C.T. Jackson proceeded to Hospital suffering from face sores. Two men of this battalion were detailed to assist local farmer with Harvesting.	
13th.	2nd Lieut. H.E. Ward returned with 17 men and servant from the Lewis Gun Course at Etaples. Two men of this battalion were detailed to assist local Farmer with Harvesting.	
14th	2nd Lieut. H.E. Ward took charge of Lewis Gun Section. Lieut. S.H.D. Faulkner returned to the Transport from Hospital. Lieut. Barton-Smith "A" Company came in to LOUEZ from the trenches.	
15th	2nd Lieut. S.H. Bailey posted to No. 10 Platoon "C" Company and proceeded to the trenches. P.1634 Sgt. R. Roe, "B" Company transferred to "D" Company and proceeded to the trenches.	
16th.	2nd Lieut. H.N.C. Chase admitted to Hospital suffering from P.U.O. Sentence on No. P.70 Pte. W. Kenyon commuted to 3 months Field Punishment No. 1. 1 Sgt. and 7 men of "D" Company's platoon at rest returned to duty i in the Trenches.	

Army Form C. 2118.

WAR DIARY
or
INTELLIGENCE SUMMARY.
(Erase heading not required.)

Instructions regarding War Diaries and Intelligence Summaries are contained in F.S. Regs., Part II. and the Staff Manual respectively. Title pages will be prepared in manuscript.

Hour, Date, Place	Summary of Events and Information	Remarks and references to Appendices
September 17th.	The Platoons of "A", "C" and "D" Companies returned to the trenches to duty. Platoons out for rest :- "B" Company No. 7 Platoon under 2nd Lieut. R. Hodgkinson. "C" Company No 11 Platoon under 2nd Lieut. J.J. Tinker. "D" Company No 13 Platoon under Lieut. C.D.M. Keyworth and 2nd Lieut. H.P. Muckleston.	
18th	Lieut. F. Barton-Smith with servant and Sgt. R.M. Chadwick proceeded to 3rd Army Infantry School on Course of Instruction. C.S.M. F.R. Rowlands "B" Company reported at Headquarters, LOUEZ, to temporarily take up duties of Regimental Sergeant Major. Capt: G.W. Parkinson transferred from "C" Company and proceeded to BOIS de BRAY as O.C. 17th Corps Light Railway. Lieut. P.H. Pettiford proceed from ARIANE to MAISON BLANCHE to be attached temporarily for duty with "A" Company.	
19th	Major W. Longbottom (transferred to "C" Company 17th) proceeded to NEUVILLE ST VAASTE to take up his duties. 2nd Lieut. R. Hodgkinson transferred to 3rd Field Survey Company. R. Royal Engineers reported to-day.	
20th	Lecture at 3 p.m. by Major McCall, D.A.A. & Q.M.G. 60th (London) Division, on Self Inflicted and Accidental Injuries and Court Martial. Commanding Officer and 12 Officers attended. Corporal A.S. Stockton accidentally wounded in leg by Lewis Gun. 2nd Lieut. A.M. Pawsey came in to LOUEZ from "A" Company for rest.	

Army Form C. 2118.

WAR DIARY
or
INTELLIGENCE SUMMARY.
(Erase heading not required.)

Instructions regarding War Diaries and Intelligence Summaries are contained in F.S. Regs., Part II. and the Staff Manual respectively. Title pages will be prepared in manuscript.

Hour, Date, Place	Summary of Events and Information	Remarks and references to Appendices
September 21st	No. P.819 Pte. J.E. Waters "C" Company killed in Left Sector. Capt. G.L. Thornton, R.A.M.C. Medical Officer returned to duty with 2/6th London Field Ambulance. Capt. Hardcastle reported to take over duties as Medical Officer.	
22nd	No. P.819 Pte J.. Waters buried in Cemetery at LOUEZ. Service by Roman Catholic Padre. Rev. Father Kennedy, 181st Infantry Brigade. The detachment on special duty at La Targette returned to duty with their Companies to-day. 2nd Lieut. B. Moore came in to LOUEZ from La Targette for rest.	
23rd	2nd Lieut. P.P. Butters and 5 men returned to LOUEZ from Lewis Gun School, Etaples. 2nd Lieut. H.P. Muckleston left LOUEZ with 5 men to proceed to the Lewis Gun School at Etaples. 2nd Lieut. A.M. Pawsey returned to duty with "A" Company in the Trenches.	
24th	The Platoons of "B", "C" and "D" Companies at rest returned to duty in the trenches. Platoons out for rest :- "A" Company No. 4 Platoon under 2nd Lieuts. G. Wood and E.H. Treacy. "C" Company No. 9 Platoon (Platoon Officer, Mr Moore already in at rest). "D" Company No. 14 Platoon under 2nd Lieut. R.W. Williams.	

WAR DIARY
or
INTELLIGENCE SUMMARY.
(*Erase heading not required.*)

Army Form C. 2118.

Hour, Date, Place	Summary of Events and Information	Remarks and references to Appendices
September 24th	Commanding Officer came in to LOUEZ from ARIANE for rest. Major Buckley 2nd in Command left LOUEZ for ARIANE to take over duties	
27th	No. P. 134 Sgt. J.R. Allen was tried by F.G.C.M. charged with "Negligence - Wounding a Comrade". The finding of the Court was "Not Guilty".	

Army Form C. 2118.

WAR DIARY
or
INTELLIGENCE SUMMARY.
(Erase heading not required.)

Instructions regarding War Diaries and Intelligence Summaries are contained in F.S. Regs., Part II and the Staff Manual respectively. Title pages will be prepared in manuscript.

Hour, Date, Place	Summary of Events and Information	Remarks and references to Appendices
	SUMMARY OF MONTH'S WORK IN TRENCHES.	

Dug-outs.
    Brigade Signal Dug-out — Completed.
    Dug-out at L.20   do
    Dug-out at F.1.   do
    Dug-outs in Progress.   16.

Work done on Dug-outs in Progress —
    11 Landing Frames.
    13 Flying Traverses
    24 Gallery Frames   } Put in Place.
    3 Bomb Traps
    62 Dug-out Frames

    2 Large Trench Mortar Emplacements completed
    2 Small   do   do   do
    4 Small   do   do   Practically complete.
    3 Sump Holes Dug.
    56 Revetting Frames Erected.
    757 Yards Trench Deepened
    30 Yards Trench Drained.
    234 Yards Trench Revetted
    2 Fire Bays Completed
    1298 Feet Duckboards laid.

Army Form C. 2118.

WAR DIARY
or
INTELLIGENCE SUMMARY.
(*Erase heading not required.*)

Instructions regarding War Diaries and Intelligence Summaries are contained in F.S. Regs., Part II. and the Staff Manual respectively. Title pages will be prepared in manuscript.

Hour, Date, Place	Summary of Events and Information	Remarks and references to Appendices
	The following Officers proceeded on Courses :-	
3rd Army Infantry School. AUXI LE CHATEAU.	Lieut. F. Barton-Smith and 1 N.C.O. proceeded on 17th Sept. 1916.	
Lewis Gun School. LE TOUQUET.	2nd Lieut. H.E. Ward and 17 O.R. proceeded on 6th Sept.	
	2nd Lieut. P.P. Butters and 4 O.R. proceeded on 14th Sept.	
	2nd Lieut. H.P. Muckleston and 4 O.R. proceeded on 23rd Sept.	
	2nd Lieut. G. Wood and 4 O.R. proceeded on 30th Sept.	

(73989) W4141—463. 400,000. 9/14. H.&J.Ltd. Forms/C. 2118/10.

Army Form C. 2118.

WAR DIARY
or
INTELLIGENCE SUMMARY.
(Erase heading not required.)

Hour, Date, Place	Summary of Events and Information	Remarks and references to Appendices
	CASUALTIES - September 1st to 30th.	
	4 Officers admitted to Hospital - Sick.	
	1 Officer Transferred to Royal Engineers.	
	60 Other Ranks admitted to Hospital - Sick.	
	1 do Killed.	
	2 do sent to Base for Dental Treatment.	
	3 do do unfit for Service at the Front.	
	3 do do under age.	
	Regimental Sergeant Major sent to Base for Transfer to England.	
	49 Other Ranks returned to duty.	
	TOTAL STRENGTH - SEPTEMBER 30th 1916.	
	42 Officers - 751 Other Ranks.	

Instructions regarding War Diaries and Intelligence Summaries are contained in F.S. Regs., Part II. and the Staff Manual respectively. Title pages will be prepared in manuscript.

Army Form C. 2118.

WAR DIARY
or
INTELLIGENCE SUMMARY.
(*Erase heading not required.*)

Confidential

War Diary
of
1/12th Bn. Royal North Lancs. Regt. (Pioneer)

from 1st September to 30th September 1916.

(Volume 4)

WAR DIARY
or
INTELLIGENCE SUMMARY.
(Erase heading not required.)

Army Form C. 2118.

Hour, Date, Place	Summary of Events and Information	Remarks and references to Appendices
1916. September 1st.	2/Lieuts. H.S. Lewis and H.P. Muckleston reported for duty at LOUEZ from the Reserve Battalion at Oswestry. 3 men reported for duty from a Cold Shoeing Course and were sent to the Transport Lines.	
3rd.	2/Lieuts. H.S. Lewis and H.P. Muckleston were posted to "D" Company and proceeded to duty in the Trenches at ECURIE. The platoons of "A", "C" and "D" Companies at rest returned to the Trenches and were replaced at LOUEZ by No. 1 platoon of "A" Company under 2nd Lieut. J.M. McCorquodale, No. 3 platoon of "B" Company attached to "C" Company, under Lieut. J.B.B. Solger and 2nd Lieut. C.A. Young, No. 10 platoon of "C" Company under Lieut. A. Gillespie and No. 15 platoon of "D" Company under 2nd Lieut. W.T. Heizes. Sentence on No. 22,290 L/Col. D. Seaside, 2/3rd Royal Dublin Fusilier 6 months Hard Labour. Commuted to 2 months Field Punishment No. 1. Promulgated at 11.15 a.m. to-day. Lieut. F. Barton-Smith came out to rest. Lieut. R.T. Powell, "A" Company came out from the Trenches to-day for rest.	
4th.		
6th.	Major W. Longbottom came in to LOUEZ from "D" company for rest. 2nd Lieut. H.E. Ward proceeded with 17 men and servant on Lewis Gun Course at Le Touquet, Etables. No. 3656 R.S.M. Connor M.C. left LOUEZ to report to No. 25 Infantry	

Army Form C. 2118.

WAR DIARY
or
INTELLIGENCE SUMMARY.
(Erase heading not required.)

Instructions regarding War Diaries and Intelligence Summaries are contained in F.S. Regs., Part II. and the Staff Manual respectively. Title pages will be prepared in manuscript.

Hour, Date, Place	Summary of Events and Information	Remarks and references to Appendices
September 6th (Contd)	Base Depot, ETAPLES.	
8th	Lieut. F. Barton-Smith "A" Company returned to duty in the Trenches.	
9th	No. P.70 Pte. W. Kenyon was tried by F.G.C.M. on a charge of "Using insubordinate language to his superior officer".	
	Two men of this battalion were detailed to assist local farmer with Harvesting.	
10th.	2nd Lieut. S.H. Bailey was sent to the Transport Lines to assist Lieut. J. White during the absence of Lieut. S.H.D. Faulkner, - sick.	
	The platoons of "A", "B", "C" and "D" companies at rest returned to duty in the trenches.	
	Platoons out for rest :-	
	"A" Company No. 2 Platoon under 2nd Lieut. E.J. Hart.	
	"C" Company No 12 Platoon under 2nd Lieuts. G. Bryers and H.N.C. Chase.	
	"D" Company No 16 Platoon under 2nd Lieut. H.S. Lewis.	
	Major W. Longbottom came in to LOUEZ from ARIANE and proceeded to Hospital suffering from P.U.O.	
11th	Sentence on No. P.70 Pte. W. Kenyon - 12 months Hard Labour. Promulgated to-day.	
	1 Officer and 32 men of No. 15 Platoon "D" Company and 1 Officer and 24 men of No. 4 Platoon "A" Company proceeded to LA TARGETTE under 2nd Lieut. B. Moore.	

Army Form C. 2118.

WAR DIARY
or
INTELLIGENCE SUMMARY.
(Erase heading not required.)

Instructions regarding War Diaries and Intelligence
Summaries are contained in F.S. Regs., Part II.
and the Staff Manual respectively. Title pages
will be prepared in manuscript.

Hour, Date, Place	Summary of Events and Information	Remarks and references to Appendices
September 12th.	Major W. Longbottom returned to LOUEZ from Hospital.	
	2nd Lieut. C.F. Jackson proceeded to Hospital suffering from face sores.	
	Two men of this battalion were detailed to assist local farmer with Harvesting.	
13th.	2nd Lieut. H.B. Ward returned with 17 men and servant from the Lewis Gun Course at Etaples.	
	Two men of this battalion were detailed to assist local Farmer with Harvesting.	
14th	2nd Lieut. H.B. Ward took charge of Lewis Gun Section.	
	Lieut. S.H.D. Faulkner returned to the Transport from Hospital.	
	Lieut. Barton-Smith "A" Company came in to LOUEZ from the trenches.	
15th	2nd Lieut. S.H. Bailey posted to No. 10 Platoon "C" Company and proceeded to the trenches.	
	P.1634 Sgt. R. Roe, "B" Company transferred to "D" Company and proceeded to the trenches.	
16th.	2nd Lieut. H.N.C. Chase admitted to Hospital suffering from P.U.O.	
	Sentence on No: P.70 Pte. W. Kenyon commuted to 3 months Field Punishment No. 1.	
	1 Sgt. and 7 men of "D" Company's platoon at rest returned to duty in the Trenches.	

(73989) W4141—463. 400,000. 9/14. H.&J. Ltd. Forms/C. 2118/10.

Army Form C. 2118.

WAR DIARY
or
INTELLIGENCE SUMMARY.
(Erase heading not required.)

Instructions regarding War Diaries and Intelligence Summaries are contained in F.S. Regs., Part II. and the Staff Manual respectively. Title pages will be prepared in manuscript.

Hour, Date, Place	Summary of Events and Information	Remarks and references to Appendices
September 17th.	The Platoons of "A", "C" and "D" Companies returned to the trenches to duty. Platoons out for rest :- "B" Company No. 7 Platoon under 2nd Lieut. R. Hodgkinson. "C" Company No 11 Platoon under 2nd Lieut. J.J. Pinker. "D" Company No 13 Platoon under Lieut. C.D.M. Keyworth and 2nd Lieut. H.P. Muckleston.	
18th	Lieut. F. Barton-Smith with servant and Sgt. R.M. Chadwick proceeded to 3rd Army Infantry School on Course of Instruction. C.S.M. F.R. Rowlands "B" Company reported at Headquarters, LOUEZ, to temporarily take up duties of Regimental Sergeant Major. Capt. G.W. Parkinson transferred from "C" Company to "B" Company and proceeded to Bois de Bray as o.c. 17th Corps Light Railway. Lieut. F.A. Pettiford proceed from ARIANE to MAISON BLANCHE to be attached temporarily for duty with "A" Company. Major W. Longbottom (transferred to "C" Company 17th) proceeded to NEUVILLE ST VAASTE to take up his duties.	
19th	2nd Lieut. R. Hodgkinson transferred to 3rd Field Survey Company. M. Royal Engineers reported to-day.	
20th	Lecture at 3 p.m. by Major McCall, D.A.A. & Q.M.G. 60th (London) Division, on Self Inflicted and Accidental Injuries and Court Martial. Commanding Officer and 12 Officers attended. Corporal A.S. Stockton accidentally wounded in leg by Lewis Gun. 2nd Lieut. A.M. Pawsey came in to LOUEZ from "A" Company for rest.	

(73989) W4141—463. 400,000. 9/14. H.&J.Ltd. Forms/C. 2118/10.

Army Form C. 2118.

WAR DIARY
or
INTELLIGENCE SUMMARY.
(Erase heading not required.)

Instructions regarding War Diaries and Intelligence Summaries are contained in F.S. Regs., Part II. and the Staff Manual respectively. Title pages will be prepared in manuscript.

Hour, Date, Place	Summary of Events and Information	Remarks and references to Appendices
September 21st	No. P.619 Pte. J.W. Waters "C" Company killed in Left Sector. Capt. G.L. Thornton, R.A.M.C. Medical Officer returned to duty with 2/6th London Field Ambulance. Capt. Hardcastle reported to take over duties as Medical Officer.	
22nd	No. P.619 Pte J.W. Waters buried in Cemetery at LOUEZ. Service by Roman Catholic Padre, Rev. Father Kennedy, 181st Infantry Brigade. The detachment on special duty at La Targette returned to duty with their Companies to-day. 2nd Lieut. B. Moore came in to IDUEZ from La Targette for rest.	
23rd	2nd Lieut. P.P. Butters and 5 men returned to LOUEZ from Lewis Gun School, Etaples. 2nd Lieut. H.P. Muckleston left LOUEZ with 5 men to proceed to the Lewis Gun School at Etaples. 2nd Lieut. A.M. Pawsey returned to duty with "A" Company in the Trenches.	
24th	The Platoons of "B", "C" and "D" Companies at rest returned to duty in the trenches. Platoons out for rest :- "A" Company No. 4 Platoon under 2nd Lieuts. G. Wood and B.H. Treacy. "C" Company No. 9 Platoon (Platoon Officer, Mr Moore already in at rest). "D" Company No. 14 Platoon under 2nd Lieut. R.W. Williams.	

Army Form C. 2118.

WAR DIARY
or
INTELLIGENCE SUMMARY.
(*Erase heading not required.*)

Instructions regarding War Diaries and Intelligence Summaries are contained in F. S. Regs., Part II. and the Staff Manual respectively. Title pages will be prepared in manuscript.

Hour, Date, Place	Summary of Events and Information	Remarks and references to Appendices
September 24th	Commanding Officer came in to LOUEZ from ARIANE for rest. Major Buckley 2nd in Command left LOUEZ for ARIANE to take over duties	
27th	No.1 P., 134 Sgt. J.K. Allen was tried by F.G.C.M. charged with "Negligence – Sounding a Comrade". The finding of the Court was "Not Guilty".	

Army Form C. 2118.

Instructions regarding War Diaries and Intelligence Summaries are contained in F.S. Regs., Part II. and the Staff Manual respectively. Title pages will be prepared in manuscript.

WAR DIARY
or
INTELLIGENCE SUMMARY.

(Erase heading not required.)

Hour, Date, Place	Summary of Events and Information	Remarks and references to Appendices
	SUMMARY OF MONTH'S WORK IN TRENCHES.	
Dug-outs.	Brigade Signal Dug-out — Completed.	
	Dug-out at L.20 do	
	Dug-out at P.1. do	
	Dug-outs in Progress. 16.	
	Work done on Dug-outs in Progress —	
	11 Landing Frames.	
	13 Flying Traverses	
	24 Gallery Frames } Put in Place.	
	3 Bomb Traps	
	62 Dug-out Frames	
	2 Large Trench Mortar Emplacements completed	
	2 Small do do	
	4 Small do do Practically complete.	
	3 Sump Holes Dug.	
	56 Revetting Frames Erected.	
	757 Yards Trench Deepened	
	30 Yards Trench Drained.	
	234 Yards Trench Revetted	
	2 Fire Bays Completed	
	1238 Feet Duckboards laid.	

(73989) W4141—463. 400,000. 9/14. H.&J.Ltd. Forms/C. 2118/10.

Army Form C. 2118.

WAR DIARY
or
INTELLIGENCE SUMMARY.
(*Erase heading not required.*)

Hour, Date, Place	Summary of Events and Information	Remarks and references to Appendices
	The following Officers proceeded on Courses :-	
3rd Army Infantry School, AUXI LE CHATEAU.	Lieut. F. Barton-Smith and 1 N.C.O. proceeded on 17th Sept. 1918.	
Lewis Gun School, LE TOUQUET.	2nd Lieut. H.E. Ward and 17 O.R. proceeded on 6th Sept.	
	2nd Lieut. P.P. Butters and 4 O.R. proceeded on 11th Sept.	
	2nd Lieut. H.P. Muckleston and 4 O.R. proceeded on 23rd Sept.	
	2nd Lieut. G. Wood and 4 O.R. proceeded on 30th Sept.	

Army Form C. 2118.

WAR DIARY
or
INTELLIGENCE SUMMARY.
(Erase heading not required.)

Hour, Date, Place	Summary of Events and Information	Remarks and references to Appendices
	September 1st to 30th.	

CASUALTIES -

    4 Officers admitted to Hospital - Sick.
    1 Officer Transferred to Royal Engineers.
  60 Other Ranks admitted to Hospital - Sick.
    1   do   Killed.
    2   do   Sent to Base for Dental Treatment.
    3   do   do   unfit for Service at the Front.
    3   do   do   under age.
  Regimental Sergeant Major sent to Base for Transfer to England.

  49 Other Ranks returned to duty.

TOTAL STRENGTH - ~~NONE~~ SEPTEMBER 30th 1916.

    42 Officers - 751 Other Ranks.

Army Form C. 2118.

WAR DIARY
or
INTELLIGENCE SUMMARY.
(*Erase heading not required.*)

Confidential

War Diary

of

1/12th Bn. Loyal North Lancs Regt (Pioneers)

from 1st October to 31st October 1916.

(Volume 5)

Army Form C. 2118.

WAR DIARY
or
INTELLIGENCE SUMMARY.
(Erase heading not required.)

Instructions regarding War Diaries and Intelligence Summaries are contained in F.S. Regs., Part II. and the Staff Manual respectively. Title pages will be prepared in manuscript.

Hour, Date, Place	Summary of Events and Information	Remarks and references to Appendices
October 1st.	The Platoons of "A", "C" and "D" Companies now at rest returned to duty in the Trenches. Platoons out to rest :- "A" Company No. 1 Platoon under 2nd Lieut. G.M. McCorquodale "C" Company No 10 Platoon under Lieut. A. Gillespie and 2nd Lt S.H. Bailey, and 2nd Lt S.N. Bradbury x "D" Company No 15 Platoon under 2nd Lieut. W.F. Hedges. Captain M. Montgomery and Captain J.M. Marshall returned to Trenches to-day.	
3rd	Captain D.N. Hardcastle, R.A.M.C. departed and Captain A.J.C. Tingey R.A.M.C. reported as Medical Officer and was taken on the strength of the Battalion.	
4th	The Commanding Officer proceeded to England on Leave. Major A. Buckley, 2nd in Command returned to LOUEZ from ARIANE to take over duties. Major W. Longbottom left NEUVILLE ST VAASTE and proceeded to ARIANE to take over duties.	
5th	Captain J.P. Bayley reported at Headquarters, LOUEZ from Hospital.	
6th	2nd Lieut. C.T. Jackson reported at Headquarters, LOUEZ from Hospital. The Platoons of "A", "C" and "D" Companies now at rest returned to duty in the Trenches.	

Army Form C. 2118.

WAR DIARY
or
INTELLIGENCE SUMMARY.
(Erase heading not required.)

Instructions regarding War Diaries and Intelligence Summaries are contained in F.S.Regs., Part II. and the Staff Manual respectively. Title pages will be prepared in manuscript.

Hour, Date, Place	Summary of Events and Information	Remarks and references to Appendices
October 6th	Platoons out to rest :- "A" Company No. 2 Platoon under 2nd Lieuts. A.M. Pawsey & E.J. Hart. "B" Company No. 3 Platoon under Lieut. J.E.S. Bodger & 2nd Lieuts. G. Bryers and C.A. Young. "D" Company No. 16 Platoon under Captain Watters & 2nd Lieut. H.S. Lewis In accordance with instructions received at 9 p.m. "Gas Alert" position assumed at 9.30 p.m. Cancelled at 10 p.m.	
7th	"Gas Alert" Signal received again at 12-45 a.m. All in the Alert position in 10 minutes. Cancelled at 1.15 a.m. The G.O.C., Division, inspected Regimental Transport. In accordance with instructions received at 7.30 p.m. "Gas Alert" position assumed at 8.15 p.m. Cancelled at 9 p.m. 2nd Lieut. H.E. Ward in temporary Command of Lewis Gun Section at Headquarters returned to duty in the Trenches with "D" Company. 2nd Lieut. J.G. Wood and 4 men returned from Lewis Gun Course.	
8th	In accordance with instructions received at 8 p.m. "Gas Alert" position assumed at 8.45 p.m. Cancelled at 9.30 p.m. 2nd Lieut. J.G. Wood returned to duty in the Trenches with "A" Company. 2nd Lieut. E.J. Hart and 4 men left for Lewis Gun Course at Le Touquet. Lieut. P.H. Pettiford came in to Headquarters for rest.	
9th	2nd Lieut. J.C.T. Jackson and 24 Lewis Gun Men proceeded to the Left Sector for Special Work.	

Army Form C. 2118.

WAR DIARY
or
INTELLIGENCE SUMMARY.
(Erase heading not required.)

Instructions regarding War Diaries and Intelligence Summaries are contained in F.S. Regs., Part II. and the Staff Manual respectively. Title pages will be prepared in manuscript.

Hour, Date, Place	Summary of Events and Information	Remarks and references to Appendices
October 10th	Captain J.P. Bayley, O.C., "A" Company returned to duty in the Trenches. Lieut. R.T. Powell "A" Company came in to Headquarters for rest. 7 men departed and proceeded to Base for transfer to 16th (Irish) Division.	
11th	The Platoons of "A", "B" and "D" Companies now at rest returned to duty in the Trenches. Platoons out to rest :- "B" Company No. 7 Platoon under 2nd Lieut. P.P. Butters. "C" Company No 12 Platoon under 2nd Lieut. G. Bryers, *already out* "D" Company No 13 Platoon under 2nd Lieut. R.W. Williams.	
12th	The Band of the 181st Brigade visited us and played selections from 11 a.m. to 12.30 noon. This is to be repeated weekly. Court of Enquiry re loss of fittings of "C" Company Camp Cooker re-assembled at 2 P.M. President - Captain J.M. Turnbull. Members - Lieut. R.T. Powell. 2nd Lt. W.T. Hedges.	
13th	Court of Enquiry re loss of 3 Ground Sheets from "D" Company's Camp Cooker re-assembled at 2 p.m. President - Captain J.M. Turnbull. Members - Lieut. R.T. Powell. Lieut. P.H. Pettiford.	

Army Form C. 2118.

WAR DIARY
or
INTELLIGENCE SUMMARY.
(Erase heading not required.)

Instructions regarding War Diaries and Intelligence Summaries are contained in F.S. Regs., Part II and the Staff Manual respectively. Title pages will be prepared in manuscript.

Hour, Date, Place	Summary of Events and Information	Remarks and references to Appendices
October 13th	2nd Lieut. H.S. Lewis and 20 men of "D" Company transferred from Right to Left Sector for Special Work.	
14th	Captain M. Montgomery O.C., "D" Company came in to Headquarters to prepare to proceed on Course at 3rd Army Infantry School. Captain A.J.C. Tingey, R.A.M.C., Medical Officer left to-day to report to A.D.M.S. 60th (London) Division. Captain D.N. Hardcastle R.A.M.C. again took over the duties of Medical Officer.	
15th	P.1162 Pte. S. Jones "C" Company was tried by F.G.C.M. at Headquarters 181st Infantry Brigade, ETRUN, charged with "When on Active Service disobeying a lawful command given by his superior officer, in that he in the Reserve Trenches on 9th October 1916 did not go back to his work of cleaning out dug-outs when ordered to do so by P.723 Sgt. M.N.Gallpen." Captain M. Montgomery and C.S.M. J. Harper proceeded on Course to 3rd Army Infantry School, AUXI LE CHATEAU. The Commanding Officer reported back from leave in England, having arrived at BOULOGNE on 14th instant and reporting at Divisional Headquarters onroute.	
16th	The platoons of "B", "C" and "D" Companies now at rest returned to duty in the trenches.	

Army Form C. 2118.

WAR DIARY
or
INTELLIGENCE SUMMARY.
(Erase heading not required.)

Instructions regarding War Diaries and Intelligence Summaries are contained in F. S. Regs., Part II. and the Staff Manual respectively. Title pages will be prepared in manuscript.

Hour, Date, Place	Summary of Events and Information	Remarks and references to Appendices
October 16th	Platoons out to rest :-	
	"A" Company No. 4 Platoon under 2nd Lieut. E. H. Treacy.	
	"C" Company No 11 Platoon under 2nd Lieuts. B. Moore & J. J. Tinker.	
	"D" Company No 14 Platoon under 2nd Lieut H. P. Muckleston.	
	Sentence on No. P.1162 Pte. S. Jones viz. 42 Days Field Punishment No. 1, promulgated at 4.19. p.m.	
	Major A. Buckley and Lieut. P.H. Pettiford returned to duty at Advanced Headquarters at ARIANE.	
	Major M. Longbottom came in to LOUEZ from ARIANE for rest.	
18th	2nd Lieut. G. Wood "A" Company came in to LOUEZ for rest.	
20th	2nd Lieut. A.K. Sadler reported at LOUEZ for duty with this Battalion from the 4th Border Regiment.	
21st	The Platoons of "A", "C" and "D" Company now at rest returned to duty in the Trenches.	
	Platoons out to rest :-	
	"A" Company No. 1 Platoon under 2nd Lieut. G. M. McCorquodale.	
	"C" Company No. 9 Platoon under 2nd Lieut. S. N. Bradbury.	
	"D" Company No. 15 Platoon under 2nd Lieut H. E. Ward.	
	"Galert" Signal received at 12.15 noon. All men at Headquarters assumed Alert position taking 15 minutes. Platoons coming in to rest were warned on arrival. Cancelled at 4.30 p.m.	
23rd	Captain M. Montgomery was admitted into Hospital from 3rd Army Infantry School.	

Army Form C. 2118.

WAR DIARY
or
INTELLIGENCE SUMMARY.
(Erase heading not required.)

Instructions regarding War Diaries and Intelligence Summaries are contained in F.S. Regs., Part II. and the Staff Manual respectively. Title pages will be prepared in manuscript.

Hour, Date, Place	Summary of Events and Information	Remarks and references to Appendices
October 24th	All Companies were withdrawn from the Trenches (including the Company from 17th Corps Light Railway at BOIS de BRAY) as and when relieved by 3rd Canadian Division Pioneers.	
25th	Battalion marched away from LOUEZ at 10.15 a.m. and proceeded via ETRUN, ARRAS-ST POL ROAD, HAUTE AVESNES, SAVY, PENIN, MAZIERES to GOUY en TERNOIS arriving at 7 p.m.	
28th	Battalion marched away from GOUY en TERNOIS at 8 a.m. and proceeded via ETREE WAMIN, REBREUVIETTE to CANTELEUX. C and D Companies were billeted at BEAUVOIR. A and B Companies with Headquarters (including specialists) were billeted at CANTELEUX. ALL arrived at destination at 1.30 P.M.	
29th	Battalion Marched away from CANTELEUX at 9.30 a.m. C and D Companies (from BEAUVOIR) joined the column at BARLY. 10.30. All arrived at BOISBERGUES at 12.30 p.m.	
30th	2nd Lieut. H.N.C. Chase reported for duty from Hospital.	
31st	General Court Martial held at Boisbergues on Capt. P. Bayley of this Battalion Charge. Drunkenness while on Active Service.	

Army Form C. 2118.

WAR DIARY
or
INTELLIGENCE SUMMARY.
(*Erase heading not required.*)

Hour, Date, Place	Summary of Events and Information	Remarks and references to Appendices
	The following Officers proceeded on Courses during the month :-	
3rd Army Infantry School AUXI LE CHATEAU.	Captain M. Montgomery and 1 N.C.O. proceeded on 15th Oct., 1916.	
Lewis Gun School, LE TOUQUET.	2nd Lieut. E.J. Hart and 3 O.R. proceeded on 8th Oct., 1916.	
	2nd Lieut. C.T. Jackson and 3 O.R. proceeded on 16th Oct., 1916.	
	2nd Lieut. G. Bryers and 3 O.R. proceeded on 24th Oct., 1916.	
Trench Cookery Course, 60th Divisional Convalescent Company.	L/Cpl J. Wakeling proceeded on 11th Oct., 1916.	

Instructions regarding War Diaries and Intelligence Summaries are contained in F.S. Regs., Part II. and the Staff Manual respectively. Title pages will be prepared in manuscript.

Army Form C. 2118.

WAR DIARY
or
INTELLIGENCE SUMMARY.
(Erase heading not required.)

Instructions regarding War Diaries and Intelligence Summaries are contained in F.S. Regs., Part II. and the Staff Manual respectively. Title pages will be prepared in manuscript.

Hour, Date, Place	Summary of Events and Information	Remarks and references to Appendices
	CASUALTIES - October 1st to 31st.	
	1 Officer and 30 Other Ranks admitted to Hospital - Sick-	
	2 Other Ranks Wounded.	
	1 O.R. Died of Wounds.	
	3 Officers and 30 Other Ranks returned to duty from Hospital.	
	8 Other Ranks Transferred to Irish Division.	
	4 do sent to base for Dental Treatment.	
	2 do do under age.	
	1 do do unfit for duty at the front.	
	TOTAL STRENGTH - 31st OCTOBER 1916.	
	42 Officers - 737 Other Ranks.	

Army Form C. 2118.

WAR DIARY
or
INTELLIGENCE SUMMARY.
(Erase heading not required.)

Instructions regarding War Diaries and Intelligence Summaries are contained in F.S.Regs., Part II. and the Staff Manual respectively. Title pages will be prepared in manuscript.

Hour, Date, Place	Summary of Events and Information	Remarks and references to Appendices
	SUMMARY OF MONTH'S WORK IN TRENCHES.	
	Dug-outs. Denis le Rock Dug-out Completed.	
	Birkin Dug-out do	
	Devon Dug-out do	
	Lassale Dug-out do	
	Chassery Dug-out do	
	Dug-outs in Progress — 3	
	Work done on Dug outs in Progress.	
	17 Landing Frames ⎫	
	30 Gallery Frames ⎬ Put in Place.	
	50 Dug-out Frames ⎪	
	6 Entrance Frames ⎪	
	29 Revetting Frames ⎭	
	3 Trench Mortar Emplacements — Completed.	
	2 Trench Mortar Emplacements — in progress.	
	12 Yards Trench Revetted.	

Army Form C. 2118.

WAR DIARY
or
INTELLIGENCE SUMMARY.
(Erase heading not required.)

Vol 5

Hour, Date, Place	Summary of Events and Information	Remarks and references to Appendices

Confidential

War Diary

of

1/12th Bn. Royal North Lancs Regt (Pioneers)

from 1st October to 31st October 1916.

(Volume 5)

Instructions regarding War Diaries and Intelligence Summaries are contained in F. S. Regs., Part II. and the Staff Manual respectively. Title pages will be prepared in manuscript.

Army Form C. 2118.

WAR DIARY
or
INTELLIGENCE SUMMARY.
(Erase heading not required.)

Instructions regarding War Diaries and Intelligence Summaries are contained in F.S. Regs., Part II. and the Staff Manual respectively. Title pages will be prepared in manuscript.

Hour, Date, Place	Summary of Events and Information	Remarks and references to Appendices
October 1st.	The Platoons of "A", "C" and "D" Companies now at rest returned to duty in the Trenches. Platoons out to rest:- "A" Company No. 1 Platoon under 2nd Lieut. S.W. McCorquodale "C" Company No 10 Platoon under Lieut. A. Gillespie and 2nd Lt. S.F. Bailey, and 2nd Lt S.W. Bradoury x"D" Company No 15 Platoon under 2nd Lieut. W.F. Hodges. Captain W. Montgomery and Captain J.W. Marshall returned to Trenches to-day.	
3rd	Captain D.N. Hardcastle, R.A.M.C. departed and Captain A.S.C. Tinley R.A.M.C. reported as Medical Officer and was taken on the strength of the Battalion.	
4th	The Commanding Officer proceeded to England on Leave. Major A. Buckley, 2nd in Command returned to LOUEZ from ARIANE to take over duties. Major S. Longbottom left GRUVILLE ST VAACTE and proceeded to ARIANE to take over duties.	
5th	Captain J.P. Bavley reported at Headquarters, LOUEZ from Hospital. 2nd Lieut. C.T. Jackson reported at Headquarters, LOUEZ from Hospital.	
6th	The Platoons of "A", "C" and "D" Companies now at rest returned to duty in the Trenches.	

Army Form C. 2118.

WAR DIARY
or
INTELLIGENCE SUMMARY.
(Erase heading not required.)

Instructions regarding War Diaries and Intelligence Summaries are contained in F.S.Regs., Part II. and the Staff Manual respectively. Title pages will be prepared in manuscript.

Hour, Date, Place	Summary of Events and Information	Remarks and references to Appendices
October 6th	Platoons out to rest :-	
	"A" Company No. 2 Platoon under 2nd Lieuts. A.C. Pawsey & E.J. Hart.	
	"B" Company No. 6 Platoon under Lieut. J.E.S. Rodger & 2nd Lieuts. F. Bryers and C.A. Young.	
	"D" Company No. 15 Platoon under Captain Watters & 2nd Lieut. H.S.Lewis	
7th	In accordance with instructions received at 9 p.m. "Gas Alert" position assumed at 9.30 p.m. Cancelled at 10 p.m.	
	"Gas Alert" Signal received again at 12-45 a.m. All in the Alert position in 10 minutes. Cancelled at 1.15 a.m.	
	The J.O.C. inspected Regimental Transport.	
	In accordance with instructions received at 7.20 p.m. "Gas Alert" position assumed at 8.15 p.m. Cancelled at 9 p.m.	
	2nd Lieut. H.E. Ward in temporary Command of Lewis Gun Section at Headquarters returned to duty in the Trenches with "D" Company.	
	2nd Lieut. J.T. Wood and 4 men returned from Lewis Gun Course.	
8th	In accordance with instructions received at 8 p.m. "Gas Alert" position assumed at 8.45 p.m. Cancelled at 9.20 p.m.	
	2nd Lieut. J. Wool returned to duty in the Trenches with "A" Company.	
	2nd Lieut. E.J. Hart and 4 men left for Lewis Gun Course at Le Touquet.	
9th	Lieut. P.H. Pettifori came in to Headquarters for rest.	
	2nd Lieut. C.T. Jackson and 24 Lewis Gun Men proceeded to the Left Sector for Special Work.	

Army Form C. 2118.

WAR DIARY
or
INTELLIGENCE SUMMARY.
(Erase heading not required.)

Instructions regarding War Diaries and Intelligence Summaries are contained in F.S. Regs., Part II. and the Staff Manual respectively. Title pages will be prepared in manuscript.

Hour, Date, Place	Summary of Events and Information	Remarks and references to Appendices
October 10th	Captain J.P. Tayler, O.C., "A" Company returned to Hd., in the Trenches. Lieut. R.E. Powell "A" Company came into Headquarters for test. 7 men reported and proceeded to Base for transfer to 18th (Irish) Division.	
11th	The Platoons of "A", "B" and "C" Companies now at rest returned to duty in the Trenches. "Platoons out to rest":— "B" Company No. 7 Platoon under 2nd Lieut. P.P. Butters; "C" Company No 12 Platoon under 2nd Lieut. E. Greory *(already out)* "D" Company No 13 Platoon under 2nd Lieut. R.M. Millam.	
12th	The Band of the 131st Brigade visited us and played selections from 11 a.m. to 12.00 noon. This is to be repeated weekly. Court of Enquiry re loss of Kitting of "C" Company Camp Cooker re-assembled at 2 P.M. President — Captain J.W. Turnbull. Members — Lieut. F.R. Powell. 2nd Lt. R.F. Eades.	
13th	Court of Enquiry re loss of 2 Ground Sheets ("A" "D" Company's Camp Cooks re-assembling at 3 p.m.). President — Captain J.W. Turnbull. Members — Lieut. R.R. Powell. Lieut. P.H. Petaford.	

Army Form C. 2118.

WAR DIARY
or
INTELLIGENCE SUMMARY.
(Erase heading not required.)

Instructions regarding War Diaries and Intelligence Summaries are contained in F.S. Regs., Part II and the Staff Manual respectively. Title pages will be prepared in manuscript.

Hour, Date, Place	Summary of Events and Information	Remarks and references to Appendices
October 13th	2nd Lieut. A.S. Lewis and 20 men of "D" Company transferred from Right to Left Sector for Special Work. Captain M. Montgomery O.C. "D" Company came in to Headquarters to prepare to proceed on Course at 3rd Army Infantry School.	
14th	Captain A.J.C. Finney, R.A.M.C., Medical Officer left to-day to revert to A.D.M.S. 60th (London) Division. Captain C.N. Hardcastle R.A.M.C. again took over the duties of Medical Officer.	
15th	P.4162 Pte. S. Jones "C" Company was tried by F.G.C.M. at Headquarters 131st Infantry Brigade, ETRUN, charged with "When on Active Service disobeying a lawful command given by his superior officer, in that he in the Reserve Trenches on 9th October 1916 did not go back to his work of cleaning out dug-outs when ordered to do so by P.722 Sgt. M.N. Callben. Captain M. Montgomery and Capt. J.E. Mercer proceeded on Course to 3rd Army Infantry School, AUXI LE CHATEAU. The Commanding Officer reported back from leave in England, having arrived at BOULOGNE on 14th instant and reporting at Divisional Headquarters onroute.	
16th	The platoons of "B", "C" and "D" Companies now at rest returned to duty in the trenches.	

Army Form C. 2118.

WAR DIARY
or
INTELLIGENCE SUMMARY.
(Erase heading not required.)

Instructions regarding War Diaries and Intelligence Summaries are contained in F.S. Regs., Part II. and the Staff Manual respectively. Title pages will be prepared in manuscript.

Hour, Date, Place	Summary of Events and Information	Remarks and references to Appendices
October 18th	Platoons out to rest :-	
	"A" Company No. 4 Platoon under 2nd Lieut. E.A. Treacy;	
	"C" Company No 11 Platoon under 2nd Lieuts. B. Moore & J.J. Tinker.	
	"D" Company No 14 Platoon under 2nd Lieut. H. P. Muckleston.	
	Sentence on No. P.1162 Pte. S. Jones viz. 42 Days Field Punishment No. 1, promulgated at 4.10 p.m.	
	Major A. Buckley and Lieut. P.H. Pettiford returned to duty at Advanced Headquarters at ARIANE.	
	Major M. Longbottom came in to LOUEZ from ARIANE for rest.	
19th	2nd Lieut. G. Wood "A" Company came in to LOUEZ for rest.	
20th	2nd Lieut. A.K. Sadler reported at LOUEZ for duty with this Battalion from the 4th Border Regiment.	
21st	The Platoons of "A", "C" and "D" Company now at rest returned to duty in the Trenches.	
	Platoons out to rest :-	
	"A" Company No. 1 Platoon under 2nd Lieut. G.M. McCorquodale.	
	"C" Company No. 9 Platoon under 2nd Lieut. S.N. Bradbury.	
	"D" Company No. 15 Platoon under 2nd Lieut H.S. Ward.	
	"Alert" Signal received at 12.45 noon. All men at Headquarters assumed Alert position taking 15 minutes. Platoons coming in to rest were warned on arrival. Cancelled at 4.20 p.m.	
23rd	Captain M. Montgomery was admitted into Hospital from 3rd Army Infantry School.	

Army Form C. 2118.

WAR DIARY
or
INTELLIGENCE SUMMARY.
(Erase heading not required.)

Instructions regarding War Diaries and Intelligence Summaries are contained in F.S. Regs., Part II. and the Staff Manual respectively. Title pages will be prepared in manuscript.

Hour, Date, Place	Summary of Events and Information	Remarks and references to Appendices
October 24th	All Companies were withdrawn from the Trenches (including the Company from 17th Corps Light Railway at BOIS de BRAY) as and when relieved by 3rd Canadian Division Pioneers.	
25th	Battalion marched away from LOUEZ at 10.15 a.m. and proceeded via ETRUN, ARRAS-ST POL ROAD, HAUTE AVESNES, SAVY, PENIN, MAZIERES to GOUY en TERNOIS arriving at 7 p.m.	
28th	Battalion marched away from GOUY en TERNOIS at 8 a.m.; and proceeded via ETREE WAMIN, REBREUVIETTE to CANTELEUX.; C and D Companies were billetted at BEAUVOIR.; A and B Companies with Headquarters (including specialists) were billetted at CANTELEUX. All arrived at destination at 1.30 p.m.	
29th	Battalion Marched away from CANTELEUX at 9.30 a.m.; C and D Companies (from BEAUVOIR) joined the column at BARLY. 10.30 All arrived at BOISBERGUES at 12.30 p.m.	
30th	2nd Lieut. H.N.C. Chase reported for duty from Hospital.)	
31st	General Court Martial held at Doorbergues on Capt J.P.Bayley of this Battalion Charge. Drunkenness while on Active Service	

Army Form C. 2118.

WAR DIARY
or
INTELLIGENCE SUMMARY.
(Erase heading not required.)

Instructions regarding War Diaries and Intelligence Summaries are contained in F.S. Regs., Part II. and the Staff Manual respectively. Title pages will be prepared in manuscript.

Hour, Date, Place	Summary of Events and Information	Remarks and references to Appendices
	The following Officers proceeded on Courses during the month :-	
3rd Army Infantry School AUXI LE CHATEAU.	Captain M. Montgomery and 1 N.C.O. proceeded on 15th Oct., 1916.	
Lewis Gun School. LE TOUQUET.	2nd Lieut. T.D. Hart and 3 O.R. proceeded on 8th Oct., 1916.	
	2nd Lieut. C.F. Jackson and 3 O.R. proceeded on 16th Oct., 1916.	
	2nd Lieut. G. Bryers and 3 O.R. proceeded on 24th Oct., 1916.	
Trench Cookery Course. 20th Divisional Convalescent Company.	L/Cpl J. Keeling proceeded on 11th Oct., 1916.	

Army Form C. 2118.

WAR DIARY
or
INTELLIGENCE SUMMARY.
(Erase heading not required.)

Instructions regarding War Diaries and Intelligence Summaries are contained in F.S. Regs., Part II. and the Staff Manual respectively. Title pages will be prepared in manuscript.

Hour, Date, Place	Summary of Events and Information	Remarks and references to Appendices
	CASUALTIES - October 1st to 31st.	
	1 Officer and 29 Other Ranks admitted to Hospital - Sick-	
	2 Other Ranks Wounded.	
	4 O.R. Died of Wounds.	
	3 Officers and 20 Other Ranks returned to duty from Hospital.	
	2 Other Ranks Transferred to Irish Division.	
	4 do sent to base for Dental Treatment.	
	2 do do under age.	
	1 do do unfit for duty at the Front.	
	TOTAL STRENGTH - 31st OCTOBER 1916.	
	42 Officers - 737 Other Ranks.	

Army Form C. 2118.

WAR DIARY
or
INTELLIGENCE SUMMARY.
(Erase heading not required.)

Instructions regarding War Diaries and Intelligence Summaries are contained in F.S. Regs., Part II. and the Staff Manual respectively. Title pages will be prepared in manuscript.

Hour, Date, Place	Summary of Events and Information	Remarks and references to Appendices
	SUMMARY OF MONTH'S WORK IN TRENCHES.	
	Dug-outs. Denis le Rock Dug-out — Completed.	
	Birkin Dug-out — do	
	Devon Dug-out — do	
	Lassale Dug-out — do	
	Chassery Dug-out — do	
	Dug-outs in Progress — 8	
	Work done on Dug outs in Progress.	
	17 Landing Frames	
	90 Gallery Frames	
	50 Dug-out Frames } Put in Place.	
	6 Entrance Frames	
	29 Revetting Frames	
	3 Trench Mortar Emplacements — Completed.	
	2 Trench Mortar Emplacements — in progress.	
	12 Yards Trench Revetted.	

ATTACHED 32nd Divisional Pioneers

Joined from 60th Division (via G.H.Q.)
   16.11.16.

1/12th BATTALION

LOYAL NORTH LANCASHIRE REGIMENT

NOVEMBER 1916

Army Form C. 2118.

WAR DIARY
or
INTELLIGENCE SUMMARY.
(Erase heading not required.)

Instructions regarding War Diaries and Intelligence Summaries are contained in F.S. Regs., Part II. and the Staff Manual respectively. Title pages will be prepared in manuscript.

Hour, Date, Place	Summary of Events and Information	Remarks and references to Appendices
November 1st	The Battalion was stationed at BOISBERGUES. Captain G.W. Parkinson reported back at midnight from duty with the 17th Corps Light Railway.	
2nd	2nd Lieut. J.G. Bryers and 4 Other Ranks reported from Lewis Gun Course.	
3rd	The Battalion marched from BOISBERGUES via BERNAVILLE and DOMESMONT to RIBEAUCOURT.	
4th	The Battalion marched from RIBEAUCOURT via ERGNIES and FAMECHON to AILLY le HAUT CLOCHER. "C" and "D" Companies were billetted at FAMECHON and "A" and "B" and Headquarters were billetted at AILLY le HAUT CLOCHER. C.S.M. Cooper. G.W. 2/17th Bn. London Regiment reported to the Battalion at AILLY le HAUT CLOCHER and is appointed Battalion Sergeant Major.	
5th	The Battalion left the 60th (London) Division and marched from AILLY le HAUT CLOCHER via FAMECHON, DOMQUEUR, CRAMONT, CONTEVILLE to HEIRMONT where we had instructions to billet but found all billets occupied by R.A.M.C. and A.S.C.; so the Battalion billetted at BERNATRE.	
6th	The Battalion left BERNATRE and marched via AUXI le CHATEAU, Le PONCHEL, FONTAINE d' ETALON, VACUERIETTE, HESDIN to WAMIN. The Battalion was attached to G.H.Q. Troops.	
10th	Major A. Buckley and Major W. Longbottom proceeded on leave to England.	
13th	Sentence on Captain J.P. Bayley, "Dismissed the Service" promulgated at 8.30 a.m. He left for England at 9.15 a.m.	

Army Form C. 2118.

WAR DIARY
or
INTELLIGENCE SUMMARY.
(Erase heading not required.)

Instructions regarding War Diaries and Intelligence Summaries are contained in F. S. Regs., Part II. and the Staff Manual respectively. Title pages will be prepared in manuscript.

Hour, Date, Place	Summary of Events and Information	Remarks and references to Appendices
November 16th	The Battalion marched away from WAMIN at 5.30 a.m. Entrained at HESDIN and moved off at 8.20 a.m. arriving at ALBERT about 5.30 p.m. The Battalion had instructions to billet at AVELUY but these were cancelled and in accordance with further orders received we billetted at ENGLEBELMER at 1-30 a.m.	
17th	The Battalion joined the 32nd Division. The Battalion was inspected by the G.O.C. 32nd Division. Reinforcement of 73 men reported.	
18th	The Battalion moves from ENGLEBELMER to Camp 1½ Kilometres west of MAILLY MAILLET. "B", "C" and "D" Companies sent out working parties to the trenches at night. "B" Company remained in the trenches and "C" and "D" Companies returned at 4.30 a.m. 19th inst. Captain G.W. Parkinson transferred to 144th Army Troops Company R.E. Authority A.G's A/18829 and 5th Army A/666/988. Reinforcement of 107 men reported.	
19th	"A", "C" and "D" Companies moved out to meet guides at level crossing AUCHON VILLERS Station, but no guides arrived at 8 p.m. as arranged, so the Companies returned to camp at 11 p.m. 2nd Lieut. G.W. McCorquodale and 30 men proceeded to BERTRANCOURT to erect huts at Divisional Headquarters.	
20th	"B" Company returned to Camp from the trenches to-day.	

Army Form C. 2118.

WAR DIARY
or
INTELLIGENCE SUMMARY.
(Erase heading not required.)

Instructions regarding War Diaries and Intelligence Summaries are contained in F.S. Regs., Part II. and the Staff Manual respectively. Title pages will be prepared in manuscript.

Hour, Date, Place	Summary of Events and Information	Remarks and references to Appendices
November 20th	"A", "C" and "D" Companies went out for 4 hours work at night digging new front line trench (NEW MUNICH TRENCH) in front of BEAUMONT HAMEL, Returning at 4.30 a.m.; 21st.	
21st	Major A. Buckley and Major W. Longbottom reported back from leave. "A", "C" and "D" Companies went out for 4 hours work at night digging NEW MUNICH Trench in front of BEAUMONT HAMEL, returning at 3.30 a.m.; 22nd Captain H. Wilkinson was appointed O.C. "A" Company and took over duties.;	
22nd	Major W. Longbottom took over duties of Adjutant from Captain H. Wilkinson.: "A" Company moved into billets at AUCHON VILLERS at 2 p.m. During night of 22—23rd "A", "B", "C" and "D" Companies all provided working parties for completing new fire trench in front of BEAUMONT HAMEL One O.R. Wounded.; 2nd Lieut. G. Bryers admitted into Hospital — Sick.	
23rd	"D" Company moved into billets at AUCHON VILLERS.; "A", "B" and "D" Companies provided working parties for completing front line trench in front of BEAUMONT HAMEL. 2 O.R. Killed. 7 O.R. Wounded. Captain G.W. Parkinson proceeded on leave to England.	
24th	"A", "B" and "D" Companies all provided working parties for new front line trench at BEAUMONT HAMEL.	

WAR DIARY or INTELLIGENCE SUMMARY.

(Erase heading not required.)

Army Form C. 2118.

Hour, Date, Place	Summary of Events and Information	Remarks and references to Appendices
November 24th	"C" Company provided working party for Light Railway from AUCHON Villers to BEAUMONT HAMEL.	
25th	The 7th Division took over from the 32nd Division. This Battalion was left behind and temporarily attached to the 7th Division. No work done to-day, men resting. Captain M. Montgomery proceeded on leave to England. The C.R.E. 7th Division called and allotted this Battalion the work of the upkeep of the roads to and around BEAUMONT HAMEL, and the upkeep and extension of the Light Railways on the Divisional Front. Work on Roads allotted to "A" and "D" Companies and work on Light Railways allotted to "B" and "C" Companies.	
26th	"A" and "D" Companies carried on work all day repairing road through BEAUMONT HAMEL Village. "B" and "C" Companies were employed about camp cleaning up and erecting Armstrong Huts.	
27th & 28th	"A" and "D" Companies worked on roads in BEAUMONT HAMEL under Major "A" Buckley. "B" and "C" Companies worked on Light Railways between MAILLY MAILLET, AUCHON VILLERS and BEAUMONT HAMEL.	
27th	Lieut. F. Barton-Smith proceeded on leave to England.	
29th	Work carried on as per previous day. 3 Other Ranks Wounded. Lieut. & Q'mr G.D. Chambers proceeded on leave to England.	
30th	Work on Roads and Light Railways as before.	

Army Form C. 2118.

WAR DIARY
or
INTELLIGENCE SUMMARY.
(*Erase heading not required.*)

Instructions regarding War Diaries and Intelligence Summaries are contained in F. S. Regs., Part II. and the Staff Manual respectively. Title pages will be prepared in manuscript.

Hour, Date, Place	Summary of Events and Information	Remarks and references to Appendices
November 30th	Captain J.M. Turnbull left to report to the Town Major, ARRAS for instruction in the duties of Town Major. Authority 5th Army letter V.A./284/166 Dated 26/11/16.	

Army Form C. 2118.

WAR DIARY
or
INTELLIGENCE SUMMARY.
(Erase heading not required.)

Instructions regarding War Diaries and Intelligence Summaries are contained in F.S. Regs., Part II and the Staff Manual respectively. Title pages will be prepared in manuscript.

Hour, Date, Place	Summary of Events and Information	Remarks and references to Appendices
	CASUALTIES — November 1st to 30th:	
	1 Officer and 76 Other Ranks admitted to Hospital — Sick.	
	13 Other Ranks — Wounded.	
	2 Other Ranks — Killed.	
	1 Other Rank — Died of Wounds.	
	1 Officer and 13 Other Ranks returned to duty from Hospital.	
	1 Other Rank sent to Base under age.	
	TOTAL STRENGTH — 30th November 1916.	
	42 Officers — 891 Other Ranks.	

(73989) W4141—463. 400,000. 9/14. H.&J.Ltd. Forms/C. 2118/10.

ATTACHED   32nd Divisional Pioneers

1/12th BATTALION

LOYAL NORTH LANCASHIRE REGIMENT

DECEMBER 1 9 1 6

> 1/12 Bn. LOYAL N. LANCS. REGT.
> (PIONEERS.)
> -1 JAN. 1917
> No. B/1/11/8/17

To Headquarters
 32 Division

I beg to forward herewith War Diary of this Battalion, for the Month of December 1916

W Loughton
Major

In the Field
1st January 1917 for O/C 1/12TH BN. L. N. LANCS. REGT. (PIONEERS)

Army Form C. 2118.

WAR DIARY
or
INTELLIGENCE SUMMARY.
(Erase heading not required.)

Vol 7

Confidential

War Diary
of
1/12th Bn Loyal North Lancs Regt (Pioneers)
from 1st December to 31st December 1916

(Volume 7)

Army Form C. 2118.

WAR DIARY
or
INTELLIGENCE SUMMARY.
(Erase heading not required.)

Instructions regarding War Diaries and Intelligence Summaries are contained in F.S. Regs., Part II. and the Staff Manual respectively. Title pages will be prepared in manuscript.

Hour, Date, Place		Summary of Events and Information	Remarks and references to Appendices
December	1st	Two Companies, "A" and "D", in Dug Outs at AUCHON VILLERS and two Companies "B" and "C" with Battalion Headquarters in Camp at MAILLY WOOD. "B" and "C" Companies employed constructing Light Railway between and about AUCHON VILLERS and BEAUMONT HAMEL. CASUALTIES – 2 O.R. Wounded. Lieut. A. Gillespie and Lieut. S.H.D. Faulkner proceeded to England on leave.	
	2nd	Work proceeded as above. CASUALTIES – 2 O.R Killed 2 O.R. Wounded.	
	3rd	Captain T. Watters proceeded to England on Leave.	
	4th	"A" Company commenced laying Water Pipe Line from SUCRERIE towards BEAUMONT HAMEL. 40 men employed. CASUALTIES – 1 O.R. Killed.	
	5th	2nd Lieut. G. BRYERS reported from Hospital. 2nd Lieut. L.A. COOKE sent to Hospital. Lieut. S.H.C. WEBSTER proceeded to England on leave.	
	6th	2nd Lieut. G. Bryers proceeded on Leave to England.	
	7th	Lieut. C.D.M. Keyworth sent to Hospital with Trench Fever. Instructions received from 5th Army through 32nd Division to strike Captain. J.M. Turnbull off the strength of the Battalion. Authority 5th Army No. A/868/996 and 32nd Division A/2278/139.	
	8th	Lieut. R.T. Powell and 2nd Lieut. P.P. Butters proceeded to England on leave.	

Army Form C. 2118.

WAR DIARY
or
INTELLIGENCE SUMMARY.
(Erase heading not required.)

Instructions regarding War Diaries and Intelligence Summaries are contained in F.S. Regs., Part II and the Staff Manual respectively. Title pages will be prepared in manuscript.

Hour, Date, Place	Summary of Events and Information	Remarks and references to Appendices
December 8th	Lieut. F. Barton-Smith reported from leave in England.	
9th	"B" Company withdrawn from work on Light Railway and started work repairing road bed for Broad Gauge Railway between COLINCAMPS and HEBUTERNE.	
10th	Lieut. and Q'mr. G.D. Chambers reported from leave in England.	
11th	2nd Lieut. B. Moore and P.597 Sgt. Crank, J.T. proceeded to MONTRELET for duty as instructors in Field Engineering at 32nd Divisional School.	
12th	Lieut. A. Gillespie and Lieut. S.H.D. Faulkner reported from leave in England.	
11th	Captain H. Wilkinson and 2nd Lieut. H.E. Ward proceeded to England on leave.	
14th	Two Platoons of "A" Company were lent to "C" Company for work on the Light Railway.	
	2nd Lieut. E.H. TREACY "A" Company, wounded by shell fire whilst employed on the Light Railway with "C" Company, and died from wounds within 1 hour in the Dressing Station at BEAUMONT HAMEL.	
	1 O.R. Wounded.	
	Captain T. Watters reported from leave in England.	
15th	The two Platoons of "A" Company which had been employed with "C" Company on the Light Railway withdrawn from AUCHON VILLERS and sent in to Camp at Battalion Headquarters MAILLY WOOD for employment on erecting NISSEN HUTS. 40 men from "A" Company under 2nd Lieut. A.M. Pawsey at AUCHON VILLERS started work on Water Pipe Line from SUCRERIE to BEAUMONT HAMEL.	

WAR DIARY
or
INTELLIGENCE SUMMARY.
(*Erase heading not required.*)

Army Form C. 2118.

Instructions regarding War Diaries and Intelligence Summaries are contained in F.S. Regs., Part II and the Staff Manual respectively. Title pages will be prepared in manuscript.

Hour, Date, Place	Summary of Events and Information	Remarks and references to Appendices
December 15th	Lieut. J. White, Lieut. J.B.S. Bodger and 2nd Lieut. G. Wood proceeded to England on leave. CASUALTIES - 1 O.R. Killed.	
16th	Lieut. S.H.C. Webster reported from leave in England.	
17th	Captain J.M. Marshall and Lieut. F.H. Pettiford proceeded to England on leave.	
19th	Lieut. R.T. Powell and 2nd Lieut. P.P. Butters reported from leave in England.	
1st to 20th	Work of Battalion proceeded as mentioned above. The Lewis Gunners were employed during this time erecting NISSEN HUTS at BOLTON CAMP, MAILLY WOOD.	
20th	All work, with the exception of erecting Nissen Huts stopped this evening preparatory to the Battalion moving out at on the 22nd. 2nd Lieut. C.T. Jackson proceeded to England on leave.	
21st	Balance of "A" and "D" Companies moved from AUCHON VILLERS to Battalion Headquarters, MAILLY WOOD. 2nd Lieut. C.A. Young proceeded on leave to England.	
22nd	Relieved by 5th Bn. South Wales Borderers (Pioneers). The Battalion marched from Camp at MAILLY WOOD at 9.30 a.m. "A" Company proceeded under the Command of Lieut. F. Barton-Smith to AMPLIER. Headquarters, and "B", "C" and "D" Companies marched to PUCHEVILLERS where the battalion went into billets. The Battalion left the 7th Division and reported to the 32nd Division on arrival at PUCHEVILLERS. 2nd Lieut. A.W. Pawsey proceeded to England on leave.	

Army Form C. 2118.

WAR DIARY
or
INTELLIGENCE SUMMARY.

(Erase heading not required.)

Instructions regarding War Diaries and Intelligence Summaries are contained in F.S. Regs., Part II. and the Staff Manual respectively. Title pages will be prepared in manuscript.

Hour, Date, Place	Summary of Events and Information	Remarks and references to Appendices
December 22nd	Captain H. Wilkinson and 2nd Lieut. H. E. Ward returned from leave.	
23rd	"B", "C" and "D" Companies spent the day cleaning arms, equipment and clothing.	
	"A" Company commenced work under orders of the C.E., 5th Corps, two platoons erecting Nissen Huts (At SARTON) and two platoons cleaning Hutment Camp at AMPLIER.	
24th	2nd Lieut. S.N. Bradbury proceeded to England on leave.	
	"D" Company commenced work as follows :-	
	One Platoons constructing Horse Standings at RUBEMPRE.	
	One Platoon constructing Horse Standings at PUCHEVILLERS.	
	Two Platoons building Bivouac Huts at PUCHEVILLERS.	
	The Lewis Gun Section commenced erecting NISSEN HUTS at MARIEUX.	
25th	CHRISTMAS DAY. All work stopped for the day except for 40 men who constructed a bath house at PUCHEVILLERS.	
	Extras were provided for the dinners for the men, and in the evening "B" and "D" Company held Company Concerts.	
	Church Parade was held on Christmas morning, the senior Chaplain of the Division taking the service.	
26th	Work resumed as on the 24th.	
	2nd Lieut. G.M. McCorquodale proceeded on leave to England.	
27th	"B" Company took over work from "D" Company in PUCHEVILLERS and RUBEMPRE.	

Army Form C. 2118.

WAR DIARY
or
INTELLIGENCE SUMMARY.
(Erase heading not required.)

Instructions regarding War Diaries and Intelligence Summaries are contained in F.S. Regs., Part II. and the Staff Manual respectively. Title pages will be prepared in manuscript.

Hour, Date, Place	Summary of Events and Information	Remarks and references to Appendices
December 27th	Orders were received from the 32nd Division for a Company to proceed to AUTHIEULE for work under the C.E., 5th Corps. "C" Company left PUCHEVILLERS for this purpose and reported in the afternoon. Major A. Buckley transferred to the 1/5th the King's (Liverpool) Regiment. Authority — A.G's A/20300 and Fifth Army A/666/1213. Lieut. J.E.S. Bodger reported back from leave.	
28th	Work proceeded as on 27th. Letter received from 32nd Division forwarding letter from G.O.C. 7th Division to G.O.C. 32nd Division. This letter read as follows :- "I wish to bring to your notice the excellent work performed by the 12th Battalion Loyal North Lancashire Regiment (Pioneers) during the time they have been attached to the Division under my Command. They have done most useful work, under great difficulties, and under conditions of considerable discomfort, and have shown a willingness and energy which merits the highest praise". (Signed) H.V. Watt. Major-General. Commanding 7th Division. 22nd December 1916. "C" Company commenced work, two platoons repairing Bivouac Hutment Camp at AUTHULE and two platoons with "A" Company repairing Bivouac Hutment Camp at AMPLIER.	

Army Form C. 2118.

WAR DIARY
or
INTELLIGENCE SUMMARY.

(*Erase heading not required.*)

Instructions regarding War Diaries and Intelligence Summaries are contained in F.S. Regs., Part II. and the Staff Manual respectively. Title pages will be prepared in manuscript.

Hour, Date, Place	Summary of Events and Information	Remarks and references to Appendices
December 29th 30th	Lieut.; P.H.; Pettiford returned from leave.; Lieut.; C.D.M.; Keyworth struck off the strength on his evacuation to England - Sick.; Authority - 5th Army No. 740/232.;	
30th & 31st.	Work continued as before.	
31st	2nd Lieut. J.J.; Tinker and 2nd Lieut.; H.S.; Lewis proceeded to England on leave.; Captain J H Marshall and 2nd Lieut.; C.J.; Jackson returned from leave.;	

(73969) W4141—463. 400,000. 9/14. H.&J.Ltd. Forms/C. 2118/10.

Army Form C. 2118.

WAR DIARY
or
INTELLIGENCE SUMMARY.
(Erase heading not required.)

Instructions regarding War Diaries and Intelligence Summaries are contained in F.S. Regs., Part II. and the Staff Manual respectively. Title pages will be prepared in manuscript.

Hour, Date, Place	Summary of Events and Information	Remarks and references to Appendices
	CASUALTIES - DECEMBER 1ST TO 31ST.	
	1 Officer and 47 Other Ranks admitted to Hospital - Sick.	
	2 Other Ranks wounded.	
	1 Officer and 2 Other Ranks died of wounds.	
	3 Other Ranks Killed.	
	1 Officer and 25 Other Ranks returned to duty from Hospital.	
	2 Other Ranks sent to Base under age.	
	TOTAL STRENGTH - 31ST DECEMBER 1916.	
	33 Officers - 345 Other Ranks.	

(73989) W 4141—463. 400,000. 9/14. H.&J.Ltd. Forms/C. 2118/10.

Army Form C. 2118.

WAR DIARY
or
INTELLIGENCE SUMMARY.
(Erase heading not required.)

Instructions regarding War Diaries and Intelligence Summaries are contained in F. S. Regs., Part II. and the Staff Manual respectively. Title pages will be prepared in manuscript.

Hour, Date, Place	Summary of Events and Information	Remarks and references to Appendices
	Confidential. War Diary of 1/12th Bn. Royal North Lancs. Regt. (Pioneers) from 1st November to 30th November 1916. (Volume 6)	

Army Form C. 2118.

WAR DIARY
or
INTELLIGENCE SUMMARY.

(Erase heading not required.)

Instructions regarding War Diaries and Intelligence Summaries are contained in F.S. Regs., Part II and the Staff Manual respectively. Title pages will be prepared in manuscript.

Hour, Date, Place	Summary of Events and Information	Remarks and references to Appendices
November 1st	The Battalion was stationed at BOISBERGUES. Captain G.W. Parkinson reported back at midnight from duty with the 17th Corps Light Railway.	
2nd	2nd Lieut. T. Bryers and 4 Other Ranks reported from Lewis Gun Course.	
3rd	The Battalion marched from BOISBERGUES via BERNAVILLE and DOMESNIL to RIBEAUCOURT.	
4th	The Battalion marched from RIBEAUCOURT via BRUNIES and FAMECHON to AILLY le HAUT CLOCHER. "C" and "D" Companies were billeted at FAMECHON and "A" and "B" and Headquarters were billeted at AILLY le HAUT CLOCHER. C.S.M. Cooper, G.W. 2/17th Bn. London Regiment reported to the Battalion at AILLY le HAUT CLOCHER and is appointed Battalion Sergeant Major.	
5th	The Battalion left the 60th (London) Division and marched from AILLY le HAUT CLOCHER via FAMECHON, DOMQUEUR, CRAMONT, CONDEVILLE to HETRMONT where we had instructions to billet but found all billets occupied by R.A.M.C. and A.S.C. so the Battalion billetted at BERNATRE.	
6th	The Battalion left BERNATRE and marched via AUXI le CHATEAU, Le BOUCHEL, FONTAINE d' ETALON, VACUERIETTE, REBEUN to WAMIN. The Battalion was attached to G.H.Q. Troops.	
10th	Major A. Buckley and Major W. Longbottom proceeded on leave to England.	
13th	Sentence on Captain J.P. Bayley, "Dismissed the Service" promulgated at 8.30 a.m. He left for England at 9.15 a.m.	

Army Form C. 2118.

WAR DIARY
or
INTELLIGENCE SUMMARY.
(Erase heading not required.)

Instructions regarding War Diaries and Intelligence Summaries are contained in F.S. Regs., Part II. and the Staff Manual respectively. Title pages will be prepared in manuscript.

Hour, Date, Place	Summary of Events and Information	Remarks and references to Appendices
November 16th	The Battalion marched away from HAMIN at 5.30 a.m. Entrained at HESDIN and moved off at 8.30 a.m., arriving at ALBERT about 5.30 p.m. The Battalion had instructions to billet at AVELUY but these were cancelled and in accordance with further orders received we billeted at ENGLEBELMER at 1-30 a.m.	
17th	The Battalion joined the 32nd Division. The Battalion was inspected by the G.O.C., 32nd Division. Reinforcement of 73 men reported.	
18th	The Battalion moved from ENGLEBELMER to Camp 14 Kilometres west of MAILLY MAILLET. "B", "C" and "D" Companies sent out working parties to the trenches at night. "B" Company remained in the trenches and "C" and "D" Companies returned at 4.30 a.m., 19th inst. Captain G.W. Parkinson transferred to 144th Army Troops Company R.E. Authority A.G's A/19829 and 5th Army A/682/298. Reinforcement of 107 men reported.	
19th	"A", "C" and "D" Companies moves out to meet guides at level crossing ACHEUX VILLAGE Station, but no guides arrived at 3 p.m. as arranged, so the Companies returned to camp at 11 p.m. 2nd Lieut. S.M. McCorquodale and 30 men proceeded to BEETRANCOURT to erect huts at Divisional Headquarters.	
20th	"B" Company returned to Camp from the trenches to-day.	

Army Form C. 2118.

WAR DIARY
or
INTELLIGENCE SUMMARY.
(Erase heading not required.)

Instructions regarding War Diaries and Intelligence Summaries are contained in F.S. Regs., Part II. and the Staff Manual respectively. Title pages will be prepared in manuscript.

Hour, Date, Place	Summary of Events and Information	Remarks and references to Appendices
November 20th	"A", "C" and "D" Companies went out for 4 hours work at night digging new Front line trench (NEW MUNICH TRENCH) in front of BEAUMONT HAMEL. Returning at 4.30 a.m. 21st.	
21st	Major A. Buckley and Major W. Longbottom reported back from leave. "A", "C" and "D" Companies went out for 4 hours work at night digging NEW MUNICH Trench in front of BEAUMONT HAMEL, returning at 2.30 a.m. 22nd.	
22nd	Captain H. Wilkinson was appointed O.C. "A" Company and took over duties. Major W. Longbottom took over duties of Adjutant from Captain H. Wilkinson. "A" Company moves into billets at AUCHON VILLERS at 2 p.m. During night of 22-23rd "A", "B", "C" and "D" Companies all provided working parties for completing new live trench in front of BEAUMONT HAMEL. One O.R. Wounded. 2nd Lieut. ?. Bryers admitted into Hospital – Sick.	
23rd	"D" Company moves into billets at AUCHON VILLERS. "A", "B" and "D" Companies provided working parties for completing Front line trench in front of BEAUMONT HAMEL. 2 O.R. Killed. 7 O.R. Wounded. Captain ?.?. Parkinson proceeded on leave to England.	
24th	"A", "B" and "D" Companies all provided working parties for new Front line trench at BEAUMONT HAMEL.	

Army Form C. 2118.

WAR DIARY
or
INTELLIGENCE SUMMARY.
(*Erase heading not required.*)

Instructions regarding War Diaries and Intelligence Summaries are contained in F. S. Regs., Part II. and the Staff Manual respectively. Title pages will be prepared in manuscript.

Hour, Date, Place		Summary of Events and Information	Remarks and references to Appendices
November	24th	"C" Company provided working party for Light Railway from AUCHON Villers to BEAUMONT HAMEL.	
	25th	The 7th Division took over from the 32nd Division. This Battalion was left behind and temporarily attached to the 7th Division. No work done to-day, men resting. Captain M. Montgomery proceeded on leave to England. The C.R.E. 7th Division called and allotted this Battalion the work of the upkeep of the roads to and around BEAUMONT HAMEL, and the upkeep and extension of the Light Railways on the Divisional Front. Work on Roads allotted to "A" and "D" Companies and work on Light Railways allotted to "B" and "C" Companies.	
	26th	"A" and "D" Companies carried on work all day repairing road through BEAUMONT HAMEL Village. "B" and "C" Companies were employed about camp cleaning up and erecting Armstrong Huts.	
	27th & 28th	"A" and "D" Companies worked on roads in BEAUMONT HAMEL under Major "A" Buckley. "B" and "C" Companies worked on Light Railways between WAILLY WAILLES, AUCHON VILLERS and BEAUMONT HAMEL. Lieut. F. Barton-Smith proceeded on leave to England.	
	29th	Work carried on as per previous day. 3 Other Ranks Wounded. Lieut. & Q'or S.C. Chambers proceeded on leave to England.	
	30th	Work on Roads and Light Railways as before.	

Army Form C. 2118.

WAR DIARY
or
INTELLIGENCE SUMMARY.

(Erase heading not required.)

Instructions regarding War Diaries and Intelligence Summaries are contained in F.S. Regs., Part II and the Staff Manual respectively. Title pages will be prepared in manuscript.

Hour, Date, Place	Summary of Events and Information	Remarks and references to Appendices
November 30th	Captain J.M. Turnbull left to report to the Town Major, ARRAS for instruction in the duties of Town Major. Authority 5th Army letter V.A./284/166 Dated 26/11/16.	

Army Form C. 2118.

WAR DIARY
or
INTELLIGENCE SUMMARY.
(Erase heading not required.)

Instructions regarding War Diaries and Intelligence Summaries are contained in F.S. Regs., Part II. and the Staff Manual respectively. Title pages will be prepared in manuscript.

Hour, Date, Place	Summary of Events and Information	Remarks and references to Appendices
	CASUALTIES — November 1st to 30th.	
	1 Officer and 76 Other Ranks admitted to Hospital — Sick.	
	13 Other Ranks — Wounded.	
	2 Other Ranks — Killed.	
	1 Other Rank — Died of Wounds.	
	1 Officer and 13 Other Ranks returned to duty from Hospital.	
	1 Other Rank sent to Base under age.	
	TOTAL STRENGTH — 30th November 1916.	
	42 Officers — 891 Other Ranks.	

1/12 Bn. LOYAL N. LANCS. REGT.
(PIONEERS.)
- 1 JAN 1917
No. B/1119/17

To/
Colonel i/c
T. F. Records
Preston.

I beg to forward herewith War Diary of this Battalion, for the Month of December 1916.

W Longbottom
Major

In the Field
1st January 1917 for O/C
1/12TH BN. L. N. LANCS. REGT. (PIONEERS)

Army Form C. 2118.

WAR DIARY
or
INTELLIGENCE SUMMARY.
(Erase heading not required.)

Summary of Events and Information	Remarks and references to Appendices
Confidential War Diary of 1/12th Bn. Royal North Lancs Regt (Pioneers) from 1st December to 31st December 1916 (Volume 4)	

Instructions regarding War Diaries and Intelligence Summaries are contained in F. S. Regs., Part II. and the Staff Manual respectively. Title pages will be prepared in manuscript.

Hour, Date, Place

Army Form C. 2118.

WAR DIARY
or
INTELLIGENCE SUMMARY.
(Erase heading not required.)

Instructions regarding War Diaries and Intelligence Summaries are contained in F.S. Regs., Part II. and the Staff Manual respectively. Title pages will be prepared in manuscript.

Hour, Date, Place	Summary of Events and Information	Remarks and references to Appendices
December 1st	Two Companies, "A" and "D", in Dug Outs at AUCHON VILLERS and two Companies "B" and "C" with Battalion Headquarters in Camp at MAILLY WOOD. "B" and "C" Companies employed constructing Light Railway between and about AUCHON VILLERS and BEAUMONT HAMEL. CASUALTIES - 2 O.R. Wounded. Lieut. A. Gillespie and Lieut. S.H.D. Faulkner proceeded to England on leave.	
2nd	Work proceeded as above.	
3rd	CASUALTIES - 2 O.R. Killed 2 O.R. Wounded. Captain T. Watters proceeded to England on Leave.	
4th	"A" Company commenced laying Water Pipe Line from SUCRERIE towards BEAUMONT HAMEL. 40 men employed. CASUALTIES - 1 O.R. Killed.	
5th	2nd Lieut. G. BRYERS reported from Hospital. 2nd Lieut. L.M. COOKE sent to Hospital. Lieut. S.H.C. WEBSTER proceeded to England on leave.	
6th	2nd Lieut. G. Bryers proceeded on Leave to England.	
7th	Lieut. C.D.M. Keyworth sent to Hospital with Trench Fever. Instructions received from 5th Army through 32nd Division to strike Captain J.M. Turnbull off the strength of the Battalion. Authority 5th Army No. A/662/996 and 32nd Division A/2278/138.	
8th	Lieut. R.B. Powell and 2nd Lieut. P.F. Butters proceeded to England on leave.	

WAR DIARY
or
INTELLIGENCE SUMMARY.

(Erase heading not required.)

Army Form C. 2118.

Hour, Date, Place	Summary of Events and Information	Remarks and references to Appendices
December 8th	Lieut. F. Barton-Smith reported from leave in England.	
9th	"B" Company withdrawn from work on Light Railway and started work repairing road bed for Broad Gauge Railway between COLINCAMPS and HEBUTERNE.	
10th	Lieut. and Q'r. G.D. Chambers reported from leave in England.	
11th	2nd Lieut. B. Moore and P.597 Sgt. Crank, J.T. proceeded to MONTRELET for duty as Instructors in Field Engineering at 32nd Divisional School.	
12th	Lieut. A. Gillespie and Lieut. S.H.D. Faulkner reported from leave in England.	
13th	Captain H. Wilkinson and 2nd Lieut. H.E. Ward proceeded to England on leave.	
14th	Two Platoons of "A" Company were lent to "C" Company for work on the Light Railway. 2nd Lieut. E.H. TREACY "A" Company, wounded by shell fire whilst employed on the Light Railway with "C" Company, and died from wounds within 1 hour in the Dressing Station at BEAUMONT HAMEL. 1 O.R. Wounded. Captain T. Watters reported from leave in England.	
15th	The two Platoons of "A" Company which had been employed with "C" Company on the Light Railway withdrawn from AUCHON VILLERS and sent in to Camp at Battalion Headquarters MAILLY WOOD for employment on erecting NISSEN HUTS. 40 men from "A" Company under 2nd Lieut. A.W. Passey at AUCHON VILLERS started work on Water Pipe Line from SUCRERIE to BEAUMONT HAMEL.	

WAR DIARY
or
INTELLIGENCE SUMMARY.
(*Erase heading not required.*)

Army Form C. 2118.

Instructions regarding War Diaries and Intelligence Summaries are contained in F.S. Regs., Part II. and the Staff Manual respectively. Title pages will be prepared in manuscript.

Hour, Date, Place	Summary of Events and Information	Remarks and references to Appendices
December 15th	Lieut. J. White, Lieut. J.E. Bodger and 2nd Lieut. G. Wood proceeded to England on leave. CASUALTIES - 1 O.R. Killed.	
16th	Lieut. S.H.C. Webster reported from leave in England.	
17th	Captain J.M. Marshall and Lieut. P.H. Pettiford proceeded to England on leave.	
19th	Lieut. R.F. Powell and 2nd Lieut. P.P. Butters reported from leave in England.	
1st to 20th	Work of Battalion proceeded as mentioned above. The Lewis Gunners were employed during this time erecting NISSEN HUTS at BOLTON CAMP, MAILLY WOOD.	
20th	All work, with the exception of erecting Nissen Huts stopped this evening preparatory to the Battalion moving out at on the 22nd. 2nd Lieut. C.T. Jackson proceeded to England on leave. Balance of "A" and "D" Companies moved from AUCHON VILLERS to Battalion Headquarters, MAILLY WOOD. 2nd Lieut. C.A. Young proceeded on leave to England.	
21st	Relieved by 5th Bn. South Wales Borderers (Pioneers). The Battalion marched from Camp at MAILLY WOOD at 9.30 a.m. "A" Company proceeded under the Command of Lieut. F. Barton-Smith to AMPLIER. Headquarters, and "B", "C" and "D" Companies marched to PUCHEVILLERS where the battalion went into billets *The battalion left the 1st Division and reported to the 32nd Division on arrival at PUCHEVILLERS*	
22nd	2nd Lieut. A.M. Pawsey proceeded to England on leave.	

Army Form C. 2118.

WAR DIARY
or
INTELLIGENCE SUMMARY.
(Erase heading not required.)

Instructions regarding War Diaries and Intelligence Summaries are contained in F. S. Regs., Part II. and the Staff Manual respectively. Title pages will be prepared in manuscript.

Hour, Date, Place		Summary of Events and Information	Remarks and references to Appendices
December	22nd	Captain H. Wilkinson and 2nd Lieut. H.B. Ward returned from leave.	
	23rd	"B", "C" and "D" Companies spent the day cleaning arms, equipment and clothing.	
		"A" Company commenced work under orders of the C.R.E. 5th Corps, two platoons erecting Nissen Huts AT BARTON and two platoons cleaning Hutment Camp at AMPLIER.	
	24th	2nd Lieut. S.N. Bradbury proceeded to England on leave.	
		"D" Company commenced work as follows:-	
		One Platoon constructing Horse Standings at RUBEMPRE.	
		One Platoon constructing Horse Standings at PUCHEVILLERS.	
		Two Platoons building Bivouac Huts at PUCHEVILLERS.	
		The Lewis Gun Section commenced erecting NISSEN HUTS at WARLEUX.	
	25th	CHRISTMAS DAY. All work stopped for the day except for 40 men who constructed a bath house at PUCHEVILLERS.	
		Extras were provided for the dinners for the men, and in the evening "B" and "D" Company held Company Concerts.	
		Church Parade was held on Christmas morning, the senior Chaplain of the Division taking the service.	
	26th	Work resumed as on the 24th.	
		2nd Lieut. J.W. McCorquodale proceeded on leave to England.	
	27th	"B" Company took over work from "D" Company in PUCHEVILLERS and RUBEMPRE.	

Army Form C. 2118.

WAR DIARY
or
INTELLIGENCE SUMMARY.
(Erase heading not required.)

Instructions regarding War Diaries and Intelligence Summaries are contained in F.S. Regs., Part II. and the Staff Manual respectively. Title pages will be prepared in manuscript.

Hour, Date, Place		Summary of Events and Information	Remarks and references to Appendices
December	27th	Orders were received from the 32nd Division for a Company to proceed to AUTHIEULE for work under the C.E. 35th Corps.	
		"C" Company left PUCHEVILLERS for this purpose and reported in the afternoon.	
		Major A. Buckley transferred to the 1/5th the King's (Liverpool) Regiment. Authority - A G's A/22330 and Fifth Army A/662/1212.	
		Lieut. J.W.S. Booper reported back from leave.	
	28th	Work proceeded as on 27th.	
		Letter received from 32nd Division forwarding letter from G.O.C. 7th Division to G.O.C. 32nd Division. This letter read as follows :-	
		"I wish to bring to your notice the excellent work performed by the 12th Battalion Loyal North Lancashire Regiment (Pioneers) during the time they have been attached to the Division under my Command."	
		"They have done most useful work, under great difficulties, and under conditions of considerable discomfort, and have shown a willingness and energy which merits the highest praise."	
		(Signed) H.V. Watts. Major-General. Commanding 7th Division.	
	22nd December 1916.		
		"C" Company commenced work, two platoons repairing Bivouac Hutment Camp at AUTHIULE and two platoons with "A" Company repairing Bivouac Hutment Camp at KEMMEL AMPLIER.	

Army Form C. 2118.

WAR DIARY
or
INTELLIGENCE SUMMARY.
(Erase heading not required.)

Instructions regarding War Diaries and Intelligence Summaries are contained in F.S. Regs., Part II. and the Staff Manual respectively. Title pages will be prepared in manuscript.

Hour, Date, Place	Summary of Events and Information	Remarks and references to Appendices
December 29th 30th	Lieut. P.H. Pettiford returned from leave. Lieut. C.D.M. Keyworth struck off the strength on his evacuation to England - Sick. Authority - 5th Army No. 740/232.	
30th & 31st.	Work continues as before.	
31st	2nd Lieut. J.J. Tinker and 2nd Lieut. H.S. Lewis proceeded to England on leave. Captain J.M. Marshall and 2nd Lieut. C.F. Jackson returned from leave.	

Army Form C. 2118.

WAR DIARY
or
INTELLIGENCE SUMMARY.
(Erase heading not required.)

Hour, Date, Place	Summary of Events and Information	Remarks and references to Appendices
	CASUALTIES - DECEMBER 1ST TO 31ST :	
	1 Officer and 47 Other Ranks admitted to Hospital - Sick.	
	2 Other Ranks wounded .	
	1 Officer and 2 Other Ranks died of wounds .	
	3 Other Ranks killed .	
	1 Officer and 25 Other Ranks returned to duty from Hospital.	
	2 Other Ranks sent to Base under age .	
	TOTAL STRENGTH - 31 ST DECEMBER 1916.	
	33 Officers - 845 Other Ranks.	

www.ingramcontent.com/pod-product-compliance
Lightning Source LLC
Chambersburg PA
CBHW081430160426
43193CB00013B/2244